385.09714 Bro

Brown, R.
Rails to the Atlantic.

(3593/sn   )

AUG 2 0 2015

W9-DBV-248

Georgina Public Libraries
90 Wexford Dr
Keswick, ON L4P 3P7

RAILS TO THE ATLANTIC

AUG 2 0 2015

RAILS TO THE ATLANTIC

EXPLORING THE RAILWAY HERITAGE
OF QUEBEC AND THE ATLANTIC PROVINCES

RON BROWN

DUNDURN
TORONTO

Copyright © Ron Brown, 2015

All rights reserved. No part of this publication may be reproduced, stored in a retrieval system, or transmitted in any form or by any means, electronic, mechanical, photocopying, recording, or otherwise (except for brief passages for purpose of review) without the prior permission of Dundurn Press. Permission to photocopy should be requested from Access Copyright.

Editor: Michael Melgaard
Design: Courtney Horner
Cover image: Ron Brown
Printer: Webcom

Library and Archives Canada Cataloguing in Publication

Brown, Ron, 1945-, author
Rails to the Atlantic : exploring the railway heritage of Quebec and the Atlantic provinces / Ron Brown.
Includes bibliographical references and index.
Issued in print and electronic formats.
ISBN 978-1-4597-2877-6 (pbk.).--ISBN 978-1-4597-2878-3 (pdf).--
ISBN 978-1-4597-2879-0 (epub)

1. Railroads--Québec (Province)--History. 2. Railroads--Atlantic Provinces--History. I. Title.

TF26.B76 2015   385.09714   C2015-902077-8
                                          C2015-902078-6

1 2 3 4 5   19 18 17 16 15

We acknowledge the support of the **Canada Council for the Arts** and the **Ontario Arts Council** for our publishing program. We also acknowledge the financial support of the **Government of Canada** through the **Canada Book Fund** and **Livres Canada Books**, and the **Government of Ontario** through the **Ontario Book Publishing Tax Credit** and the **Ontario Media Development Corporation**.

Care has been taken to trace the ownership of copyright material used in this book. The author and the publisher welcome any information enabling them to rectify any references or credits in subsequent editions.
— *J. Kirk Howard, President*

The publisher is not responsible for websites or their content unless they are owned by the publisher.

Printed and bound in Canada.

VISIT US AT
Dundurn.com
@dundurnpress
Facebook.com/dundurnpress
Pinterest.com/dundurnpress

Dundurn
3 Church Street, Suite 500
Toronto, Ontario, Canada
M5E 1M2

CONTENTS

ACKNOWLEDGEMENTS

With a work that covers such an expanse of territory as this, I needed to consult many individuals and organizations that provided assistance both with key information and with field logistics. I would like to start by thanking Gillian Hall of the Toronto office of Tourisme Quebec. She and her staff provided important contacts and generous assistance in many respects.

In the field, help was provided by many people and organizations. In no particular order, these include: Genevieve Parent of the spectacular Fairmont Chateau Frontenac in Quebec City; Debbie Starr of the historic Lord Nelson Hotel and Suites in Halifax; Denise Bradbury of the Algonquin Resort, St. Andrews by-the-Sea in New Brunswick; Glenn Bowie of the Westin Nova Scotian Hotel in Halifax; Andrew Phillips and Paul Lalonde of the Nova Scotia Museum of Industry in Stellarton; Anne Chardon of Outaouais Tourisme; Elsie Carroll of the beautiful McAdam, New Brunswick, Railway Station; Paula Wamback of the Nova Scotia Tourism Agency; Simon Leguerre of the Société de développement du Témiscamingue; Matthieu Tremblay of the Réseau Charlevoix; Marie Michele Cloutier of Les Hôtels JARO in Quebec City; Paul Bergeron of Quebec City Tourisme; Marisa Iaconelli of Tourisme Montreal; Magalie Barton of Tourisme Quebec; Louis-Antoine Paquin of CN Rail; Jennifer Burnell of Parks Canada; Alison Aiton of New Brunswick Tourism; Nathalie Beauchamp of the Fairmont Chateau Montebello; Pierre Bessette of Tourisme Quebec; Allan Bailey and Claude Chartrand of La Société d'Histoire de Senneterre; and Susan Goertzer, tour manager of Minister's Island.

I am grateful also to the proprietors of Auberge du Village in Shawville, Quebec; Auberge Eugene in Ville-Marie, Quebec; the bed and breakfast Le Voyageur in Saint-Jovite, Quebec; the New Brunswick Division of the Canadian Railroad Historical Association; the Shawville-Pontiac Historical Society; the Coastal Inn in Antigonish, Nova Scotia; and a special shout-out to my cousins Charles Millard and Paula Millard for their gracious hospitality.

INTRODUCTION

CELEBRATING THE LEGACY

The Canada we know today was largely built around railways, but how easily the country ignores that heritage. We demolish stations, we toss aside vital rail passenger service, and we have raised a younger generation that has never ridden a train.

Before the rails arrived in the 1830s, we were a widely dispersed population, clustered around ports, mill sites, farm hamlets, or, in the case of our First Nations, relegated to scattered settlements. But railways linked those places to the rest of Canada and provided access for everyone. As the rail network expanded, new communities were created. This growth was most notable across the Prairie provinces and through northern Ontario and Quebec, where entire towns appeared thanks to the railways. Speedy rail movement allowed the economy to boom. Rail towns became bustling commercial hubs.

Railway expansion lasted more than a century. The first trains began their work in the coal fields of Nova Scotia in the 1830s, using wooden steam engines that survive today in Stellarton's Museum of Industry. These industrial spurs expanded into longer rail lines that opened up large tracts of eastern Canada. Major rail lines — the National Transcontinental (NTR), the Canadian Northern (CNoR), and the Canadian Pacific (CPR) — made their way west from the east coast, while regional lines like the Intercolonial (ICR), the Grand Trunk (GTR), and the Quebec Central Railways (QCR) created a spider's web of steel throughout the hinterlands of Quebec and the Maritimes. Railway charters by the hundreds came and went, many amalgamated into or assimilated by ever-larger rail corporations. Meanwhile, the island provinces of Prince Edward Island and Newfoundland (then a colony) enjoyed their own separate rail lines.

Rail lines created a special landscape. Divisional points appeared at 150 kilometre intervals to provide assembly yards for the trains, maintenance for the engines and rolling stock, and housing for railway employees. Water towers, coal chutes, grain elevators, and warehouses became part and parcel of the emerging Canadian landscape. Everything hinged upon the railways.

Charny was a major railway hub created by the Grand Trunk Railway. The large roundhouse and yards are visible in the foreground. (Photo courtesy CN Rail.)

But the face of the railways were the stations. A city's main street often led straight up to the door of the station. Here, the rail lines put to work some the era's leading architects to create attractive, even spectacular, station buildings intended to lure travellers from competing lines. It was here, after all, that the townsfolk picked up their mail, listened to news on the station wire, bade farewell to loved ones going to war, and, if lucky, greeted them upon their return. Everything — from mail to milk to livestock to Christmas presents — was shipped from these important points.

The decline of railways began in earnest in the 1950s. Automobiles became universal, and for families, businesses, and farms, far more adaptable and convenient than the limited schedules and routes the railways provided. Modern technology made for fewer (but larger) trains that required less maintenance and eliminated the need for stations and agents every twenty kilometres.

Lines were abandoned, stations demolished, employees laid off, and passenger service virtually eliminated. Sadly, even popular tour trains were impacted by insurance rules, poor track maintenance, and ineffective marketing

Only a handful of stations survive in their original role, and these are found mostly in remote, roadless communities, such as those found in northern Quebec. Ticketing must now be done by phone or online. Except for luxurious tour trains, railway tourism opportunities are ignored. Other railway structures, once vital, have vanished from the landscape. How many water towers, coal chutes, and roundhouses survive? Scarcely any.

This work is an effort to encourage you, the reader, to celebrate the railway age — to visit the heritage railway stations that recall the golden age of rail travel. Many museums offer displays of steam engines and coaches once used to carry Canadians wherever they needed to go. Better still, board a VIA train or a tour train and enjoy a traffic-free trip. Some of eastern Canada's most dramatic scenery comes from the seat of a train coach, not a mall-lined highway.

Even lines that are now abandoned offer an opportunity to hike, cycle, or ski the old routes on some of eastern Canada's rail trails.

This book provides the first comprehensive exploration of the railway legacy of Quebec and the Atlantic provinces, and the ways in which both the modern and the railway generation can celebrate that legacy. So, "All aboard."

THE RAILS ARRIVE:
THE GROWTH OF THE RAIL NETWORK
IN QUEBEC AND THE ATLANTIC PROVINCES

While the railway age arrived in Great Britain in the 1820s, a decade would pass before rails made their way to Canada. In 1829 and 1834 horse-drawn tramways began hauling coal from the Canadian towns of New Glasgow and Sydney Mines, respectively. The lines connected the coal mining regions of the interior of Cape Breton to the coast. The Albion Railway began operating steam engines in 1838, two of which, the *Samson* and the *Albion*, are on display at the Museum of Industry in Stellarton, Nova Scotia.

In 1836 the country's first rail line opened between Lac-Saint-Jean and the St. Lawrence River across from Montreal. Using wooden rails with iron strapping, it served mainly as a portage line. The line was about twenty kilometres long and shortened the distance over which goods had to be shipped from New York City to Montreal. In 1851 the line was extended to Rouses Point, and in 1864 it was absorbed into the Grand Trunk Railway (GTR) system. A replica of one of the line's early steam locomotives, the *John Molson,* operates at Exporail in Saint-Constant, Quebec.

However, it wasn't until the 1850s that eastern Canada's railway age truly began. The GTR was chartered to link Sarnia with Portland, Maine, in 1852. This was accomplished, in part, by absorbing the existing Atlantic and St. Lawrence Railroad, which had opened in 1851 and ran from Montreal to Richmond and south to Portland. Next, the GTR took over the Quebec and Richmond Railway, which linked Richmond to Levis. By 1856 the GTR was finally running trains from Montreal to Sarnia and Portland, as well as to Levis. By 1859 the GTR's 1,530 kilometres of track made it the world's longest rail line.

But the line still required a ferry to carry passengers and freight across the St. Lawrence at Montreal. And so the Victoria Tubular Bridge (later renamed the Victoria Jubilee Bridge) was built in 1859 to span a three-kilometre crossing of the St. Lawrence. The bridge was considered an engineering marvel of its day.

But with the GTR running to Portland rather than to Halifax, both Nova Scotia and New Brunswick felt shut off from the rest of British North America, and so turned

Canada's first steam locomotive was the Samson, *built for the coal mines of Nova Scotia and now housed in the Nova Scotia Museum of Industry in Stellarton.*

to rail construction of their own. The New Brunswick and Canada Railway ran up western New Brunswick from St. Andrews to Woodstock (and eventually to Edmunston), while the European and North American Railway forged a link between Saint John, New Brunswick, and the port of Shediac. The Nova Scotia Railway opened between Halifax and Truro with branches to Windsor.

Finally, in 1867, the newly minted Canadian federal government approved the construction of a line to link the beleaguered new provinces. Oddly, since they were no longer colonies, it was called the Intercolonial Railway (ICR). By 1876 the ICR had absorbed the two regional lines and completed a link to Rivière-du-Loup on the south shore of the St. Lawrence where it met with the GTR. The ICR subsequently acquired the GTR from there to Levis, opposite Quebec City. It then took over a branch from Truro and New Glasgow in Nova Scotia to the Strait of Canso, and then became the pre-eminent rail line in the Maritimes.

Kentville was the centre of the Dominion Atlantic Railway operation in Nova Scotia, with offices housed in this large station.

The Dominion Atlantic Railway (DAR), Nova Scotia's most iconic rail line, was incorporated in 1895. It had absorbed a number of earlier lines and charters, including the West Counties Railway, the Cornwallis Valley Railway, and the Midland Railway. By the time the CPR took out a ninety-nine-year lease on the railway in 1912, the line could count forty-eight station stops between Windsor Junction and Yarmouth. The Halifax and Southwestern Railway operated on the opposite of the province, running from Halifax along the south coast also to Yarmouth. It fell into the Canadian Northern Railway (CNoR) network in 1915. Both lines are now abandoned and have become rail trails with a handful of stations and bridges still in place.

In the 1870s and 1880s Quebec began encouraging colonization rail lines of the Laurentians, often led by parish priests, to help ease congestion on the overcrowded farmlands of the St. Lawrence Valley. Colonization rail lines were built to connect the region to the rest of Quebec. These lines extended variously to Lac-Saint-Jean, to Labelle (later known as the iconic P'Tit Train du Nord), to Huberdeau, and to Waltham, where the line was known as the Pontiac and Pacific Junction Railway. Another line stretched from Hull to Maniwaki. It is now abandoned, although a small section continued to host steam excursions between Hull and Wakefield. Originally part of the Quebec Montreal Ottawa and Occidental (QMO&O) system, these colonization lines were little more than branch lines, leased by the CPR.

One of New Brunswick's key railway men was the irrepressible Alexander "Boss" Gibson. He started his empire by creating a townsite around his cotton mills at Marysville, five kilometres from Fredericton on the opposite side of the St. John River. He then put his mind to creating a railway line. Starting in 1872 he began acquiring a number of shorter rail lines, and by 1892 his network encompassed much of western New Brunswick from St. Andrews to Edmunston. In short order it was acquired by the CPR, then expanding its empire eastward.

Meanwhile, the CPR had completed its route to the west coast and was looking to expand eastward. It absorbed the DAR from Windsor Junction (its Halifax link) to Yarmouth, in western Nova Scotia. The CPR also took over the New Brunswick Railway, as well as the QMO&O along the north shore of the St. Lawrence and Ottawa Rivers and on to Ottawa with its branches into the Laurentians. Then, to complete its truly transcontinental link, the CPR acquired the charter of the Atlantic and Northwestern Railway,

enabling it to open its Short Line from the west end of Montreal, via Farnham, Sherbrooke, and Lac-Mégantic, through Maine to Saint John, New Brunswick. The charter also called for a bridge over the St. Lawrence River at Lasalle, an impressive feat of engineering that is still used today by Montreal's AMT commuter service as well as the CPR's freights. The ICR continued to expand its own network and extended its lines into Cape Breton all the way to Glace Bay, Nova Scotia.

Another addition to the growing network of rail lines was the Quebec Central Railway, which by 1895 had built lines south from Quebec City to Lac-Mégantic, and to the American border at Beebe Junction where it hooked up with the important Boston and Maine Railway.

By 1900 rail lines were everywhere, often duplicating each other. But it wasn't over yet. Two more ambitious transcontinental routes were still to come.

In 1895 a pair of railway contractors for the CPR decided to strike out on their own. They were William Mackenzie and Donald Mann. Their method was to grab up unused charters and uneconomical lines. Beginning in Manitoba, they extended their way westward to Vancouver and eastward into Ontario, Quebec, and the Maritimes, where they obtained the charter of the Quebec and Lac-Saint-Jean Railway. From a junction at Rivière-à-Pierre on that line they established a line running westerly through Shawinigan Falls, Joliette, and on to the Ontario border at Hawkesbury. They further acquired the Halifax and Southwestern Railway, which ran along the south shore of the province from Halifax to Yarmouth.

The next grand railway plan was that of the GTR and the Canadian government itself. Under the proposed scheme, the government would build and operate a new line that would travel from Moncton through Edmunston, before following the south shore of the St. Lawrence River and crossing into Quebec City over a new cantilever bridge. From there, it would angle northwest, well away from any settled area, through northern Quebec and into northern Ontario. It would then join with the Grand Trunk Pacific (GTP) at Winnipeg. But the GTP was not able to run the entire cross country route and the government took over the entire operation as the National Transcontinental Railway.

In 1871 Prince Edward Island began building a rail line of its own. But it took the involvement of the Canadian Government to finish that line as well, which was used as the catalyst to persuade Prince Edward Island to join confederation in 1875. To help reduce costs, the line was narrow gauge, the rails being only three and a half feet apart. Political pressure forced the line to twist into as many of the scattered communities as possible, resulting in 180 kilometres being built to serve a string of communities only 120 kilometres apart. The line initially ran between Charlottetown, the provincial capital, and Tidnish, the island's western terminal. By 1910 rails had been extended to Murray Harbour and the eastern terminus of Elmira. In 1915 the PEIR joined the ICR (also known as the Canadian Government Railway), which evolved shortly afterward into the CNR. However, with the arrival of the auto age, passenger service dwindled and in 1968, ended altogether. In 1989 the CNR abandoned the line and removed the tracks. Most of the route today forms the island's popular Confederation Trail. Dozens of stations survive in a variety of uses.

In 1898 the colony of Newfoundland entered the railway age as well. The idea for a rail line across the rocks of Newfoundland began with Sandford Fleming, Canada's pre-eminent railway engineer, in 1868. But it took until 1881 for the colonial government to proceed. Construction made it only one hundred kilometres, from St. John's to Whitbourne, when the builder A.L. Blackman went bankrupt and the government had to take over. In 1893 the government turned building over to Robert G. Reid, who constructed a number of branch lines, and in 1898 finally completed the line across the island to Port aux Basques.

By 1923, however, the Reid family could no longer afford the costs and the government once again took control. Following confederation with Canada in 1949, the Newfoundland Railway came under the Canadian National Railway system, which also operated the ferry links to the mainland. As usual, the beginning of the end of rails on the Rock came with the arrival of improved roads, in particular the completion of the Trans-Canada Highway in 1965. Within four years rail passenger service had ended. Onerous rate increases approved by the CTC (Canadian Transportation Commission) ultimately doomed freight service as well, and in September of 1988 Newfoundland's last train squealed to a halt in Port aux Basques. As in Prince Edward Island, the Rock was yet another province with no rail service.

Quebec's mineral resources drew new rail lines in the 1950s, with the CNR adding a loop from Saint-Félicien in the east, northwesterly to Chibougamau, and then on to rejoin the CN line at Barraute west of Senneterre. Independent from Canada's rail network and its main rail lines, the Quebec North Shore and Labrador Railway, in 1954, extended a 480 kilometre rail line from the port of Sept-Îles on the north shore of the St. Lawrence to haul iron ore from Labrador City and Schefferville. Most of the line continues to operate and offers limited passenger service to this day.

By the 1980s most of the local rail lines were gone. Much of the spider's web of lines through southern Quebec was abandoned and the rails ripped up. The provincial lines in both Prince Edward Island and Newfoundland were gone by the late 1980s.

When the CNR and the CPR decided that they no longer wished to operate passenger service on the remaining lines, VIA Rail came into existence. But it fared little better, especially in the face of hostile federal governments, both Liberal and Conservative, who discontinued the majority of its early routes. Many of its remaining routes remain underfunded and in jeopardy.

By 2015 much of eastern Canada's railway legacy was little more than a memory. Stations have been removed and roundhouses razed, leaving little evidence that the rail era even existed. However, thanks to dedicated heritage lovers, what remains of that era is now celebrated through museums, tour trains, and groomed cycling paths on the old rail lines. As well, there remain a number of railway hotels that give tourists and enthusiasts a chance to explore the very towns that the railways themselves brought to life.

BRIDGING THE GAP:
THE TRESTLES AND TUNNELS OF EASTERN CANADA

Think of railway bridges and one immediately conjures the vast chasms and looming mountains that railway structural engineers had to overcome in western Canada's mountains and the Prairies' wide valleys. But some of Canada's longest and most unusual railway bridges span the chasms and canyons of Quebec and the Atlantic provinces.

Railway engineers first built their bridges almost exclusively of wood. It was plentiful, after all, and easy to assemble. But as trains became heavier — and since wood was flammable — the use of iron and steel began to seem like a better idea. In the mid to late 1800s, a number of bridge designers came up with increasingly stronger types of bridge construction.

Truss bridges (a structure whose strength lies in the criss-crossing of lengths of wood, and later iron and steel) can be attributed to William Howe's railway bridges, built in the United States in the 1840s. Howe worked primarily with wooden structures. Squire Whipple of Utica, New York, created the first iron truss railway bridge in 1846. These gave way to increasingly stronger bridge styles from

bridge engineers like James Pratt and Thomas Warren. Terms like *deck truss* refer to trusses that are situated below the tracks, while a *through truss* lies above the tracks. An *arched* or *bowstring truss* simply refers to a bow shaped top row of steel beams. Piers were initially constructed of stone upon which *decks* (pre-manufactured sections of track) were placed. *Bents* refer to the long steel structures that support the tracks used usually in higher trestle bridges. As construction progressed, the preference for steel over iron led to bridges so durable that many remain in use today.

A *cantilever* bridge's main support extends from the ends of the structure, rather than resting on piers. They were rare in eastern Canada; however, the cantilever bridge crossing the St. Lawrence River at Quebec City is North America's longest.

THE BRIDGES OF QUEBEC

Montreal

Because the city sits on a large island in one of the

world's largest rivers, Montreal is surrounded by bridges, among them the world's greatest feats of engineering.

To the west there lie the two branches of the Ottawa River, which swirl around each side of Île Perrot. As the Grand Trunk Railway (GTR) made its way westward in the 1850s, sturdy bridges to cross these two wide waterways were needed. The bridges at Sainte-Anne-de-Bellevue and the one linking Île Perrot to Vaudreuil were completed in 1854. Designed by the firm Stephenson and Ross, the Peto Brassey Betts and Jordan Company finished the project. The bridges' sixteen piers incorporated upstream cutwaters to reduce the impact by ice floes.

The GTR initially built a tubular structure on these bridges — making them, in effect, an enclosed tunnel. That, however, proved unfeasible for a number of reasons: the bridges could not be widened to accommodate planned double tracking, the sides often caught strong gusts of wind, and the long enclosed tubes trapped smoke, making life unbearable for passengers. Finally, in 1898, the tube was replaced with an open steel deck on a row of stone piers.

Mere metres away from the GTR bridge stands the CPR bridge that was built for its main line in the 1880s. The CPR bridge uses a different style — four arched through trusses made of steel on top of a row of stone piers. These historic bridges are best viewed from the Sainte-Anne-de-Bellevue Canal National Historic Site in Sainte-Anne-de-Bellevue, over which both bridges cross.

In 1887 the CPR kept on building, adding its Short Line, from Montreal to Saint John, New Brunswick, to access the year-round port facilities. It crossed the St. Lawrence with its Lasalle Bridge. The first bridge built was a combined truss and box span. In 1908 that bridge was replaced in order to accommodate double tracking. Today's bridge uses steel deck girders and deck trusses supported on stone piers. A lift bridge over the St. Lawrence Seaway on the south shore lifts the bridge to allow the massive ocean freighters to glide by below. A small fading wooden plaque on Boulevard Lasalle in Parc Saint-Ange near the Lasalle commuter station describes the heritage of the site.

A short distance west of Sainte-Anne, the Canada Atlantic Railway (CAR) constructed a massive bridge over the St. Lawrence River in 1897, linking Valleyfield with Les Coteaux. The CAR was an ambitious project, built by Ottawa lumber baron J.R. Booth, to link the Georgian Bay port of Depot Harbour in Ontario with the Atlantic seaboard. It was opened in 1897. From Valleyfield, a one-time busy railway town and now a Montreal suburb, nine through-truss spans cross the first section of water to Île Longueil, from there four more spans link to Île aux Chats, and finally four more to Île D'Adoncourt. These structures, however, are difficult to view from anywhere but the water, and passenger trains no longer cross them. The most interesting and photogenic view from land rests in a small park in Les Coteaux, where a single-span truss carries the tracks over a crumbling abandoned lock on the old Lachine Canal.

Carrying the CNR over the Rivière-des-Prairies just beyond the Pointe-aux-Trembles station northeast of Montreal are two impressive trestles of over 350 metres and 290 metres respectively, separated by Île Boudan, with a combined total of thirteen through-arch truss spans.

But perhaps the most famous of Montreal's bridges is the Victoria Bridge. Throughout the 1850s railway building was frenzied. Tracks radiated from the south shore of the St. Lawrence, while Montreal, across the

The Canada Atlantic Railway erected a major bridge over the St. Lawrence River east of Montreal, a portion of which crosses the ruins of a Lachine Canal lock.

wide river, was fast becoming a transportation and commercial hub. Ferrying trains across the river or by winter rails on the ice was cumbersome and uneconomical. A permanent bridge from Montreal over the river was essential for trains to access the rails that linked with the Atlantic ports. And so, in 1853, the GTR hired one of the continent's most revered bridge engineers, Robert Stephenson, to come up with the impossible: a bridge over the St. Lawrence, some 2.5 kilometres

across. Three thousand workers picked up their tools and started construction.

The original design was for a tubular structure, enclosed on the sides and the top. But, as with the Sainte-Anne bridge, the design was fatally flawed. With the increasing use of coal as a fuel, the dense smoke became trapped in the tunnel. So, to no-one's surprise, the tubes were replaced in 1897–98 with a series of through trusses resting on twenty-four stone piers. It became known as the Victoria Jubilee Bridge, the longest railway bridge in the world at the time.

Modern times brought modern changes. With the auto age, the bridge was widened in 1927 to accommodate motor vehicles. Then, in 1959, with the opening of the St. Lawrence Seaway, the river rose to cover much of the iconic stone piers. In addition, a second bypass approach was added to the southern approach with a second lift bridge, so that trains might use one set of tracks while the other set rose into the air as ocean freighters passed below them.

The Quebec Bridge

This massive span of nearly six hundred metres is considered to be the world's longest cantilever railway bridge. But that engineering feat was achieved at a deadly price. Construction began in 1898, but a fatal design went unnoticed, and in 1907, as the bridge was nearing completion, the mighty structure crashed down with a roar, killing or drowning seventy-five workers. The following year, the Quebec Bridge Company took over the project, and in 1910 began the construction anew. In 1916, as the centre span was being lifted into place, the bridge collapsed again, killing thirteen. The bridge finally opened in 1917 as part of the NTR's western main line. The NTR's Bridge station stood at the north shore where VIA Rail's Sainte-Foy station now sits.

When the ICR (which later became part of the GTR) built its line between Charny and Chaudiere Junction on the west side of the Chaudiere River, it erected an impressive eight-span through-truss bridge high above the foaming rapids below.

Quebec's Northern Bridges

Many of the railways that reached into the mountains and clay plains of northern Quebec were colonization lines, built to lure settlers from the overcrowded farmlands along the St. Lawrence River Valley. The line used by the P'tit Train du Nord, constructed between 1891 and 1902, is now Quebec's most popular cycling and skiing trail, but has few significant bridges. It does, however, offer what may be the last wooden trestle in the province — an eighty-metre bridge that trail users encounter upon entering the terminus of Mont-Laurier.

The Pontiac and Pacific Junction Railway (PPJ) line constructed through the Pontiac region of Quebec, west of Aylmer, presents one fairly modest, but nonetheless historic, iron two-span through-truss bridge. Located where the trail approaches the now-silent mill town of Davidson, a short distance from Fort Coulonge. The line was completed in 1888 and abandoned in 1983. The bridge, known as the "Black Bridge," forms part of the PPJ cycling trail.

As the NTR made its way through the mountains of western and northern Quebec, the construction teams encountered many rivers and lakes that needed to be bridged. Between Hervey-Jonction and La Tuque, the tracks cross the highest trestle used by a passenger train in the province. The bridge runs over the Rivière du Milieu, and is visible only from the train. About fifty kilometres north of the divisional point of Fitzpatrick, the line crosses a system of causeways and trestles that combined extend roughly four kilometres along the Flamond River. From the divisional point and junction at Senneterre, the CNR, in 1937, extended branch lines southwesterly to Val-D'Or and Noranda to access

The deadly cantilever bridge over the St. Lawrence River at Quebec City is the world's longest cantilever bridge.

the gold and mineral deposits being extracted there. To cross a series of rivers and lakes, the CNR erected three steel bridges between Val D'Or and Noranda, all of which lie immediately beside Highway 117. The longest crosses the Thomson River, and consists of three through trusses.

The CNR didn't always enjoy success with its bridges. While constructing the three-hundred-metre bridge over the Okidodosik River, the structure had an unnerving habit of turning on its side due to the seemingly bottomless muskeg through which they were trying to build it.

The CN line to the Gaspé exhibits a string of impressive bridges, including a 230-metre structure at Grand Riviére, another of 180 metres over the river at Port-Daniel, and a 250-metre link across L'Anse-à-Beaufils River.

The Trestles

Like the bridges of western Canada, many in Quebec are high, awe-inspiring trestles above wide valleys. The famous trestle that crosses the Sainte-Ursule Falls near Shawinigan is but one. It consists of two trestles, really — one that crosses the falls themselves, which is the shorter of the two, and another, longer segment that rises high above what was once the original river bed before the course of the water was altered by an earthquake. The trestle can be seen from the footpath in Parc des Chutes de Sainte-Ursules or from the VIA train that rumbles overhead. The structure was erected by the CNoR in 1901 as part of the route between Montreal and the Lac-Saint-Jean area. The bridge stretches for three hundred metres and rises more than forty above the river below.

Such massive trestles were not just confined to the interior regions either. As the NTR edged westward from Quebec City in 1907, it followed the shore of the St. Lawrence before swinging inland to cross northern Quebec and Ontario. On what is today the outskirts of Quebec City, a massive trestle crosses the Cap Rouge River on a series of steel piers. Nearly one and a half kilometres in length, the bridge rises more than thirty metres above the river. This impressive structure is easily viewed from Rue Saint Félix or Parc de Lorraine situated at its base.

On the Mattawa to Témiscaming branch of the CPR, the trestle at Beauchesne was constructed in 1955, when the tracks were relocated to accommodate a new dam on the Ottawa River. It may not be as long as the others, but it soars more than thirty metres above the Beauchesne River. It can be seen from a logging road about thirteen kilometres southeast of the town of Témiscaming.

The CNoR Crosses the Ottawa River

In extending its line across western Quebec and into eastern Ontario, the CNoR found that it needed to cross the Ottawa River in three places. The first bridge, crossing at Hawkesbury, Ontario, no longer exists. Further west of Ottawa the line crossed the river from the Ontario side at Fitzroy Harbour into the Pontiac region of Quebec. This roughly five-hundred-metre long bridge is made up primarily of two through Pratt truss spans. The next crossing to the west was the five-hundred-metre bridge from Portage du Fort to the Ontario side. Completed in 1915, it consisted of ten deck spans and two truss spans. In 2013 the CNR announced its intention to abandon the bridges and the entire line. To view either bridge, it is necessary to walk the right of way, or venture along the river by boat.

THE BRIDGES OF NEW BRUNSWICK

The Salmon River Trestle, Grand Falls

Located east of Grand Falls, this CNR trestle stretches so far into the distance it is impossible to see one end from the other. Rising more than sixty metres above the Little Salmon River, the trestle was built by the NTR in 1914 and extends more than four kilometres across the wide valley. The best vistas of this jaw-dropping structure are from the hamlet of Davis Mill, a short distance northeast of Highway 108. CN Rail's freight trains continue to rumble across the mighty structure. At sixteen spans, it is the second longest trestle bridge in Canada. In fact, it is one of a series of four mighty trestle bridges built by the NTR within a fifty kilometre stretch east of Grand Falls.

The CN trestle over the Little Salmon River in Nova Scotia is eastern Canada's longest trestle.

The Reversing Falls Bridge, Saint John

The 1870s and 1880s saw a spate of railway construction in New Brunswick. The ICR had arrived on the east side of the Saint John River, while the New Brunswick Railway (later the CPR) halted its line on the west side. The Reversing Falls (more like reversing rapids) prevented the two lines from connecting. Because the gorge containing the falls is narrow, a fairly short bridge would do. But due to the deep and rapid flow of the river in both directions, it would not be possible to place piers in the river. In 1881 the Saint John River and Bridge Company was set up to bridge the chasm.

The final design was put forward by the Dominion Bridge Company and called for an unusual structure that used cantilevers at the ends with a suspended span between them. The cantilevers measured about eighty-five metres and one hundred and thirty metres respectively, while the centre suspended span was forty-five metres.

The overall length of the structure ended up being about four hundred metres, including approaches. It was opened for traffic in 1885. But with the increasing weight of the heavier locomotives and bigger trains, the bridge proved too light and was replaced in 1921 by a second double cantilever bridge. It remains in place today, while nearby the abutments and some piers of the original structure remain visible.

The Bill Thorpe Walking Bridge, Fredericton

It is said to be the world's longest railway walking bridge. At 581 metres, that claim is unlikely to be challenged. This nine-span through-truss bridge was built by the Fredericton and St. Mary's Railway and Bridge Company in 1886. It linked Fredericton, on the south bank of the Saint John River, to the emerging railway network on the north side, which ran from South Devon to Chatham on the ICR, as well as to Woodstock on the

Crossing the St. John River at Fredericton, the Bill Thorpe Walking Bridge is the world's largest walking bridge.

CPR. The first bridge was damaged in flooding in 1935, but was back in service two years later. By then it was under control of the CNR. That railway abandoned the line in 1996, and the bridge became part of a trail system from downtown Fredericton to Nashwaak. It functions not just as recreational trail, but also is popular with cycling commuters.

THE BRIDGES OF NOVA SCOTIA

Grand Narrows Bridge

As the ICR built its rail line across Cape Breton Island, it encountered the Bras D'Or lakes, and chose the narrows in the lake system to cross. At the time it was built in 1890, the Grand Narrows Bridge was the longest in Nova Scotia. It was built by Robert Reid (of Newfoundland Railway fame) and measured more than five hundred metres. Its seven truss spans were manufactured by the Dominion Bridge Company in Montreal and floated to the site. A swing section allows boat traffic to pass. The bridge is easily viewed from the parallel Highway 223, while the beautiful Grand Narrows Hotel nearby, which once accommodated train travellers, now offers rooms as a bed and breakfast.

CNoR's Nova Scotia Bridges

When the CNoR team of William Mackenzie and Donald Mann acquired the unfinished Halifax and Southwestern Railway in 1901 (the initials H&SW were often ridiculed to mean "Hellish Slow and Wobbly"), they needed to bridge the LaHave River at Bridgewater. Here,

The Grand Narrows Bridge in Nova Scotia opens to allow boat traffic along the scenic Bras D'or lakes.

they erected the longest bridge on the line, with six girder spans resting on stone piers. Part of the Bridgewater Centennial Trail, hikers can reach the bridge by stairs from the parking lot on King Sreet.

Another imposing CNoR bridge is the one that crosses the Mersey River in Liverpool, where the former station houses the Hank Snow Home Town Museum. Like that in Bridgewater, six steel girder spans rest on a string of piers.

THE BRIDGES OF NEWFOUNDLAND

Newfoundland: The T'Rail Bridges

When the CNR abandoned its Newfoundland route, it left behind many bridges. While most were short spans across creeks and swamps, a few exceeded thirty metres. The longest of the lot is the bridge across the Exploits River in Bishops Falls, completed in 1901 after the third attempt at doing so. Although it does not rise high above the river, its 320-metre length, consisting of four bowstring trusses, makes it the longest in that province. The bridge has new decks to facilitate trail use. Many of the smaller bridges on the line are maintained by the T'Rail commission and are used primarily by ATVs and snowmobiles.

The Trinity Loop

The strange Trinity Loop is unique in North America. Built by the Reid Newfoundland Railway on the branch line to Bonavista in 1911, it was the solution to a steep descent toward the village of Trinity. The result was a 2,012-metre track curving through 310 degrees that circled around a pond and looped ten metres under itself. After the CNR gave up on the NL Railway in 1988, the Loop became an amusement park with vintage railway equipment following the track under the bridge. By the late 1990s that too was abandoned and tracks and equipment lay unused. In 2011 Hurricane Igor caused heavy damage to the tracks. Some of the equipment, however, still rests on site, although now heavily vandalized.

Several individuals have rallied to try to rescue the derelict attraction. Even though the site is listed on the Canadian Registry of Historic Places, the province has shown little interest in helping to resurrect the unusual feature. The municipality has incorporated policies into its official plan to "encourage the redevelopment of the Trinity Loop for a commercial tourism attraction...." According to the *Canadian Trackside Guide*, the equipment consisted of a fourteen-ton diesel, a dining car, two boxcars, and a caboose.

OTHER BRIDGES

The bridge across the Tantramar Marsh leading into Sackville, New Brunswick, is a two-span arch-truss bridge on the original ICR line. What makes it interesting visually is its location immediately adjacent to an abandoned highway bridge.

The 460 metre Courcelles Bridge in Quebec's Eastern Townships is one of the few bridges maintained by a municipality as a historic structure. It was built between 1891 and 1894 by the Quebec Central Railway, and served the rail line until 1991 when the rails were lifted. The line now forms part of a rail trail, although the bridge itself, with its open ties, is barricaded.

The ICR bridge that crosses the Wallace River between Tatamagouche and Pugwash was constructed with a swing section to allow boat traffic to access the sandstone quarries upstream for export to the construction industry in Boston and New York. The structure consists of three deck spans and a through-truss span in addition to the swing span. The bridge rests on four sandstone piers and lies about ten metres above the river. Today it is part of the Trans-Canada Trail between Pugwash and Pictou and is listed on the registry of Canada's Historic Places. It is viewable only from the trail.

An impressive six-span deck-truss bridge reaches across the Salmon River in Chipman New Brunswick, built in 1907 by the Canadian Government Railway (later, the NTR) for its proposed cross Canada route from Moncton to the west coast. In the river nearby, the earlier stone pilings of the CPR are visible. The bridge remains in use by the CNR.

The CPR Short Line to Saint John, New Brunswick, crosses the Richelieu River at Saint Jean on a multi-span girder-plate bridge with a swing span in the middle to accommodate boat traffic. Near Mont Saint-Hilaire, the GTR also had a bridge across the Richelieu, and it was here that one of Canada's worst train disasters occurred. In 1864 a newly hired locomotive engineer, unfamiliar with the line's signalling system, misread a signal and plunged his passenger train into the river. Ninety-nine passengers, many of them new immigrants, perished that day. Today's bridge consists of seven deck spans.

In Newcastle, New Brunswick, a pair of long bridges cross the Miramichi and Little Miramichi Rivers respectively, both of which extended about three hundred metres and comprise five through trusses sitting on stone piers. The CPR bridge over the St. Maurice River between Cap-de-la-Madeleine and Trois-Rivières stretches nearly three hundred metres, with five through trusses resting a string of piers.

And although it is neither the longest nor the highest bridge in eastern Canada, the single-span Pratt-truss bridge over the Nine Mile River (more like a creek) in the suburban sprawl that is Elmsdale, Nova Scotia, represents Canada's oldest iron bridge. It was built in the 1870s when ICR railway builder Sandford Fleming began to insist that Canada's railways give up the practise of building wooden trestles and adopt the more durable — and fireproof — iron bridge.

THE FACE OF THE RAILWAYS: THE STATIONS

Eighteen-thirty-six marked the start of a dramatic era of rail building in eastern Canada. Hundreds of railway lines were chartered, dozens actually built. Most of them designed stations from their own "pattern books" — that is, from standard plans. The earliest designs were very similar to the stage coach hotels that preceded the railway. Stations were basically two storeys in height and constructed of wood, with little architectural embellishment. But, as railway amalgamation proceeded, so did competition. Succeeding rail companies replaced the original structures with larger and more elaborate buildings to attract more passengers. The only exceptions were in Newfoundland and in Prince Edward Island, where the railways remained under single ownerships, and where patterns were repeated across the lines with little variation.

The greatest era of station building occurred between the late 1880s and the start of the First World War. Following that war, the CNR acquired many of eastern Canada's bankrupt lines, while the CPR acquired others and added a number of their pattern-book stations.

Among the more prominent station architects were Bruce Price and the Maxwell brothers of the CPR; H.H. Richardson, an American station designer whose style of wide-arched windows and rounded features influenced many of Canada's stations; and Ralph Benjamin Pratt, a prolific architect who worked for both the CPR and the CNoR. His style typically incorporated a pyramid roofline.

In 1912 the National Transcontinental Railway (NTR), Prime Minister Wilfred Laurier's transcontinental dream, pushed westward from Moncton, across New Brunswick, and on into Quebec and Ontario before crossing the Prairies to the West Coast. It, too, used a range of standard plans, largely storey-and-a-half with hipped rooflines and embedded dormers. A few stations had two storeys, such as the one still standing in Grand Falls. This line too became part of the CNR system.

John Schofield was prominent in bringing his neoclassical style to the CNR's post–First World War stations. Sandford Fleming, while not primarily an architect, was responsible for such railway innovations as standardizing times along the railway networks and the insistence on using steel for bridge construction. The many smaller and earlier rail lines generally relied on their engineering departments for their standard station plans.

The stations were the real face of the rail lines, the point of interaction between company and customer. To embrace this relationship, the railway companies made every effort to ensure that these buildings were functionally effective and aesthetically appealing. Even the simple patterns were attractive, while with the large stations no holds were barred in obtaining the best architects and employing the grandest styles of the day.

Prior to the victory of the auto over rail travel, stations numbered in the thousands. But, as highways flourished from the 1960s onwards, and as the federal government began to feel that rail passenger service was outmoded, funding was cut and passenger service dwindled drastically. Freight operations were modernized and then computerized, requiring fewer trackside staff. Stations fell empty by the droves, and were bulldozed soon after.

Following the CPR's clandestine demolition of its distinctive West Toronto station in 1982 (despite efforts to save it) enraged Canadians led by an infuriated Toronto mayor, Art Eggleton, demanded action. Voices were raised to demand that their heritage stations be saved. Regrettably, existing laws favoured the rail companies, for they were exempt from provincial heritage laws. Only the federal government could legislate the rescue of Canada's historic stations. Surprisingly, that is what they did.

In 1988 special legislation introduced by MP Jesse Flis came into effect. Under this station-saving law, called the Heritage Railway Station Protection Act (HRSPA), stations designated by the Minister of the Environment through Parks Canada could not be demolished by the railway companies, nor could they be significantly altered.

Over several years, various ministers have designated more than three hundred stations across the nation. Of these, more than fifty are in eastern Canada. But this is still only one fifth of all those that remain on their original sites. Despite "designation," where no reuse could be found many of the stations simply rotted away or fell victim to arson.

This chapter is a guide to the more significant of eastern Canada's heritage railway stations. Those that are federally designated and still stand are all included. Many others that are listed on provincial heritage registries are also included. A few on neither list are mentioned due to their distinct heritage value.

By far, the greatest number of existing stations in eastern Canada are found in Quebec, where more than two hundred remain, and are either in use or have been preserved — many as heritage structures. Most reflect the standard patterns of their corporate owners: the Canadian Pacific, the Grand Trunk, the Intercolonial, or the Quebec Central, and a few from the Canadian Northern Railway. Of these, well over half remain on site.

MONTREAL: A CITY OF HERITAGE STATIONS

Commuter Stations

When the CPR began building commuter stations west of Montreal in 1890, it recognized that the booming

A Montreal commuter train comes to a halt at the classic CPR Vaudreuil station.

affluence of Anglophone Westmount required something extra. They employed architect W.S. Painter to devise a larger and more attractive station than the standard plans being used farther west. In 1907 the new Westmount station was opened. Built to resemble a pavilion, it boasted a pair of low, wide pyramid-roof towers to mark the ends, and a row of wide-arched windows and doorways between. Now owned by the municipality of Westmount, the brick station sits vacant, its trackside heavily overgrown. However, the more visible street side, with its wide lawn, is well maintained. Commuter trains now stop at a new shelter style station adjacent to the nearby Metro station.

Despite the neglect of the Westmount station, Montreal's western commuters can glory in an entire string of heritage CPR-era stations still in use. These include the Beaconsfield station, a brick CPR pattern with a bellcast roof adorned with a small gable; and the Valois, Vaudreuil, and Montreal West stations, all of which use various standard CPR patterns. While service to Vaudreuil–Dorion is frequent, service to a more elaborate wooden station at Hudson, on the Ottawa River, is only twice daily. The rare pattern used on the Hudson station is one of the CPR's earliest, found more commonly in northwestern Ontario. The long station, with its steep roof gable ends and row of small dormers, also serves as an arts centre and theatre.

Rigaud

Situated at the current end of the track on what was the Montreal to Ottawa south shore line, the station in Rigaud, regrettably, ended its days as a commuter station when the local municipality declined to pay its contribution to the running of the commuter service. This attractive and distinctive two-storey stone building with mansard roof was built in 1940 by the CPR at the Quebec border with Ontario on its Montreal to Ottawa south shore line to emphasize the entry into a culturally and architecturally distinctive province. It now sits vacant, although it does appear to be maintained.

Montreal's Central Station

When it was visible, Montreal's Central Station offered a handsome image of a modern International-style station. It was designed in the 1930s by CNR's main architect, John Schofield, who also designed the CNR's large station in Hamilton, Ontario. Opened in 1943, it did not remain visible for long. Within a decade, covered over by the Queen Elizabeth Hotel and other skyscrapers, it became little more than a

dimly lit subterranean concourse for shops and fast food outlets. Its railway role is limited to a few ticket counters, baggage checks, and the arrival and departure sign. It is more frequently used by commuters than inter-city travellers. Trains are not visible, as the tracks lie below the concourse.

Its few redeeming features are limited to the attractive bas-relief murals designed by Charles Comfort of Toronto, which depict Canadians at work and at play. Medallions can be found around the walls as can a bilingual version of Canada's national anthem.

Windsor Station

One would expect that William Cornelius Van Horne, the headstrong president of the CPR, would have gone for a Chateau style for his new Montreal station, which would have been keeping in line with his growing chain of hotels. Instead, he hired American architectural wonder boy

The interior of Montreal's Central Station contains bas-relief works that depict life in the Canada from the era of rail travel.

Bruce Price to create a Romanesque building not just for the Montreal station, but for CPR's corporate head office as well. But the Chateau elements were not lacking either, as evidenced by a steep roof above the upper floor. Three major additions between 1900 and 1913 kept true to Price's original theme. Its prominent entrance on Rue Saint-Antoine leads into the grand hall with the waiting room immediately to its side. The station was known as a "stub" station, where tracks ended at the waiting room.

The original structure rose four storeys, with arched windows. The additions added several storeys, marking the rail company's growing influence. But much has changed inside. The CPR moved its corporate offices to Calgary in the 1990s, while the tracks were relocated further west to serve the city's commuter rail network. Today the grand concourse is eerily silent with only footsteps echoing throughout. Most of the original doorways and woodworking mark the hall which also features a display of CPR heritage photographs.

Montreal's Windsor Station was the pride of CPR president William Cornelius Van Horne.

Dalhousie Station

Before there was Windsor Station, there was the Dalhousie Station. Here, on the site of what was prestigious Dalhousie Square (much of which burned in 1852) is the CPR's first Montreal station. The large structure is brick above a stone base in which are a row of high-arched windows. In 1883 the CPR opened the station on the site, and a year later the inaugural transcontinental train steamed out toward Vancouver. But only a few years later the grand Chateauesque Viger station/hotel (see chapter 5) opened to great acclaim, and the Dalhousie station was left in its shadow. In 1993 the Eloise Circus moved in, and 2014 saw it undergoing further renovations.

Jean-Talon

This neoclassical urban station was built in 1931 and was designed by architect Colin Drewitt. It replaced the old Mile End station used by the CPR. From this station the CPR's passenger trains steamed north into the Laurentians as well as west to Ottawa and east to Quebec City. The station closed in 1984 and served variously as a bookstore and liquor store. Designed in the Beaux-Arts style, it features a row of four pillars and a pair of columns guarding the main entrance to the waiting room. The high barrel-vaulted waiting room is illuminated by a row of tall windows with decorative curving beams, while fluted pilasters rise above the second-level mezzanine. Much of the interior still displays the marble and terrazzo of its floors and walls. Today, the former waiting room houses a Joe Fresh, where great care has been taken to preserve the three-storey room's many architectural elements. The old station still serves the travelling public as an entrance to the Montreal Metro subway system, the entrance to which leads through the former men's smoking room.

THE STATIONS OF
THE EASTERN TOWNSHIPS

From 1836 onward, Quebec's Eastern Townships endured a barrage of railway construction. Dozens of small railway companies laid out thousands of kilometres of track and erected hundreds of stations. Today, companies, tracks, and stations have largely vanished form the landscape.

Saint-Jean-sur-Richelieu (CPR)

This elegant CPR station dates to 1887, when the railway was competing to finish its line from Montreal to the Atlantic. Its features include an additional passenger canopy, a bellcast hipped roof, multiple casement arched windows with transoms, and an eyebrow vent such as are found on a number of CPR station plans. Although fenced off from the track, its exterior has remained unaltered. The building now serves as a theatre administration office and has been designated under the HRSPA.

Saint-Jean-sur-Richelieu (CN)

This brick CN station bears a remarkable resemblance to the CPR station, with its wide-hipped roof with a lower-hipped extension. Brick adornments surround the operator's bay window, as well as around the windows and doors on the street side, and rounded transoms appear over the windows and doorways. It, too, has been little altered, and serves now as a tourist office, although, like the CPR station, it is fenced from the track. It is located only a few blocks south of the CPR station. It was built by the Grand Trunk in 1891, replacing an earlier 1836 station shed, one which marked eastern Canada's oldest rail line and would have been the country's first railway station.

Sherbrooke (CPR)

Although no longer in use by the railway, Sherbrooke's CPR station remains a landmark of the city's downtown. Built in 1910, it was enlarged three times, in 1920, 1927, and around 1950. Although a single storey in height, the centre area of the operator's bay is dominated by hip cross gable in the roofline, with a secondary cross gable at the eastern end of the structure. Its large size testifies to the amount of passenger traffic, as well as its former role as a divisional station. The yards remain in use, although all other ancillary railway structures are gone. The building remains busy, housing a farmers' market known as the Marché de la Gare, as well as a deli and the Savaroso restaurant. It is also the home base of the popular Orford Express tour train, which departs from the west end of the structure.

Sherbrooke (CNR)

One of Quebec's more elegant stations, Sherbrooke's Grand Trunk station was built in 1890 after the railway had taken over the St. Lawrence and Atlantic Railway. The central section of this brick building is two storeys, with a high-peaked cross gable. Its two single-storey extensions feature hip gables at the ends. As with many of the GTR's stations of the time, the many windows feature arches. Trains no longer call, of course, although the track remains in use. The station still plays a role in the area's transportation system as a bus terminal, and contains a restaurant as well. It sits at the base of a hill, of which Sherbrooke has several, with the Hotel Wellington atop the hill behind the station.

Richmond

Shortly after the rails reached this Eastern Townships location, Richmond became a major rail hub on the key Montreal to Portland, Maine, route, and with its branch to Quebec City. In fact, its yards remain in use. The Grand Trunk built this station in 1912. The distinctive structure contains a full two-storey central portion with an octagonal two-storey bay window. Two single-storey extensions lie on either end. It is constructed of brick with carved stone lentils. Passenger service ended in the 1980s. Fenced from the track, the Richmond station now houses a motel and restaurant.

Acton Vale

The first reaction to this wonderful station is "wow." During its heyday, the GTR festooned its lines with grand upscale stations that often featured a prominent tower and decorative gables. And here, on its main

line from Montreal to Portland, Maine, the GTR designed one of its more elegant small-town stations. Completed in 1900, this wooden building features a wooden turret, dormers, a steeply pitched roof, and multi-paned windows.

The "wow" factor also derives from its state of preservation. Here, the municipality has restored the building as a tourist centre, and has carefully preserved its interior and exterior details, including washroom lettering. The tracks remain in use while a nearby bike path offers an interpretive plaque. The Acton Vale station was designated a national historic site in 1976 and is listed on the Canadian Registry of Heritage Properties.

Farnham

A postwar International-style building, this large CPR station near the vast rail yards in this busy divisional town is two storeys and displays the flat roof typical of the style. The bay window extends slightly into the second floor, but the building offers few other architectural

One of Quebec's finest station preservation efforts is the GTR station in Acton Vale.

embellishments. It was constructed in 1950 to replace an earlier structure destroyed by fire. The station is designated under the HRSPA.

Tring-Jonction

Built in 1914 shortly before the CPR assumed control of the Quebec Central Railway, the stone appearance of this station's exterior may be misleading as the material is actually moulded concrete that incorporated locally produced asbestos into its material. It is distinguished by a prominent cross gable and a porte-cochère supported by free-standing columns. The building has been renovated to serve as a local library

Vallée-Jonction

Only a few kilometres to the east of Tring-Jonction lies the unusual station at Vallée-Jonction, and it, too, is constructed of concrete moulded to resemble stone. It was built in 1917 and sits on the inside of the track junction; as a result, the station forms a "T" in three sections. A single storey in height, it also exhibits a porte-cochère and roof-line dormers. Situated on a narrow river flat below the main village, this location was a divisional point where a small roundhouse with turntable still stand. A sturdy bridge takes the tracks over the Chaudière River, while a railway display stands nearby. Once the base for the Chaudière-Appalaches tour train, the building now houses Le Musée Ferroviaire de Beauce. There is a railway hotel nearby.

East Angus

Yet a third stone-like station built by the CPR — this one in East Angus in 1913 — and leased by the Quebec Central Railway. Like the station at Tring-Jonction, East Angus has a wide hip-gabled roof and prominent gable above the operator's bay window. It now functions as a local history interpretation centre known as La Vieille Gare du Papier.

Lacolle

Americans arriving in Lacolle on the former Delaware and Hudson Railway might be forgiven for thinking that they had been suddenly transmitted to Europe, for here is a station that resembles a miniature castle. Designed by Montreal architect Charles Tetley, the station was intended to resemble a Norman manor house and give arriving visitors a preview of Quebec's architectural heritage. Built of stone in 1930, the station sports a pair of

As a port of entry, the Lacolle station provided American tourists arriving on the Delaware and Hudson Railway a taste of Quebec's architecture. It is now vacant.

conical towers that rise above a long stone structure where small dormers penetrate the steep roofline. This was formerly the customs point for arriving visitors. Now vacant, the station is owned by the municipality.

Coaticook

It would seem that border stations in the Eastern Townships of Quebec adopted particularly unusual styles. The one at Coaticook, near the U.S. border, was built by the GTR in 1904 at a time when that railway was upgrading its stations to make them more appealing. It replaced a much simpler station built on the St. Lawrence and Atlantic Railway, which linked Montreal with Portland, Maine, in 1853. The wooden building rises two storeys, with a central high gable over the operator's bay, while the waiting room offers a semi-conical roof. It is said to be the largest rounded station in eastern Canada. Passenger service ended in 1958, freight in 1980. The town purchased the station in 1988 for one dollar, remodelling the interior in 1999. In 2010 the town sold the old station to Solutions Affaires Experts-Conseils, a local business.

St. Armand

Yet another unusual border station is the one built by the Central Vermont Railway in St. Armand in 1864, making it one of Quebec's oldest surviving first-generation stations. Rising a storey-and-a-half, this Italianate brick station is identical in style to many small-town stations through the northeastern U.S., though the style is rare in Canada. Tracks were lifted in 1955, but the station,

although much altered inside, has retained its attractive exterior features.

Lac-Mégantic

It is sadly ironic that one of the few structures in Lac Mégantic to have survived the horrific explosion caused by derailed tanker cars in June of 2013 would be the station that the railway company owned. The station is one of the more attractive erected by the CPR on its tracks from Montreal to the Atlantic. Here, the operator's bay extends fully into a second storey with a hip roof. The two levels are connected by pilasters.

Built in 1926, its purpose was not just to serve the local wood industry, but also to attract tourists to the scenic region. The row of doors and windows are multi-panelled, with rounded tops surmounting the transoms. A separate transmission building dating from 1930 was linked to the main building in 1950,

The CPR-built station in Lac-Mégantic survived the fiery devastation caused by derailed tanker cars, which destroyed much of the town's core and killed many.

giving the station a rather elongated appearance. A well-maintained garden marked the street entrance. It is designated under the HRSPA.

Drummondville

VIA Rail makes only three stops between the outskirts of Quebec City and Montreal. They are at Saint-Lambert, Saint-Hyacinthe, and Drummondville. The Drummondville station was built by the GTR in 1904, and is a simple, elongated brick structure with a row of Richardsonian-style windows and doors. Although train service is frequent, VIA has removed the ticket agent, and the waiting room has become a confining, bleak hall.

Saint-Hyacinthe

Built by the GTR in 1899, this station is another example of the remarkable styles that this rail line came up with. The station has so many different elements that it is hard to categorize them. The roof is a good place to start, as it offers a high-hip cross gable with a bellcast slope extending to the street side and the two-storey operators bay. An arched portico marks the entrance to the building, while a pair of hip-gable dormers lie on either side. This brick on stone structure extends to two storeys in the centre, and a storey and a half along the extensions. While VIA Rail makes frequent daily stops, the waiting room now lacks an agent and has been reduced to a dull, featureless waiting area. In the meantime, the Mega Copie Restaurant has taken over the old waiting room, which has retained a good number of it architectural features.

Rivière-Bleue

Built in 1913 by the NTR, this nicely preserved small-town station reflects the common country station pattern of the NTR: storey-and-a-half, with steep hip roof and hip dormers in the end gable as well as atop the agent's bay window. The upper floor housed the agent's apartment. While the last passenger trains stopped coming to Rivière-Bleue in 1979, the tracks remain in use for freight service. In 1981 Le Club d'Artisanat Riverain Inc. saved the building from demolition, and for a number of years it housed a private museum. Today, it houses a museum, café, and gift shop, and is listed on the Quebec registry of heritage properties.

STATIONS OF QUEBEC'S SOUTH SHORE

Montmagny

The ICR was built as a major trunk line to link Canada's eastern provinces. The striking mansard-roofed station in Montmagny was built by that railway in 1881, one of six such structures built between Levis and Rivière-du-Loup after the ICR took over the GTR in 1873. The station in Montmagny is the sole survivor. After several decades as a CNR station, it was taken over by VIA Rail for its Atlantic routes. Cutbacks by the federal Conservatives forced the railway to remove its agent in the early 2000s.

Saint-Pascal

Although the route later became part of the ICR, several stations along the section of line from Levis to

Rivière-du-Loup were of Grand Trunk design. The station at Saint-Pascal was one, and displays a distinctive Quebecois flavour with a broad, sweeping bellcast roof that resembles many Habitant homes built at the time. The original station was built in 1856, and, according to Parks Canada, was either replicated or heavily renovated in 1913. No longer a VIA Rail stop, the building, fenced from the track, now houses community service groups.

La Pocatière

Identical to the Grand Trunk station at Saint-Pascal, the attractive yellow brick station in La Pocatière remains a VIA Rail stop on the Halifax train, although the building itself is rented out for other uses. After 2010, when the federal Conservative government forced major cutbacks on VIA, the railway removed most of its agents from smaller stations, such as at La Pocatière. Both Saint-Pascal and La Pocatière stations are designated stations under the HRSPA.

The wonderful GTR station in La Pocatière, Quebec, reflects the rural architecture of the area.

Rimouski

This relatively recent (1937) CN station shows a few more embellishments than the other, simply built stations from the period. Reflecting local architecture and a period of increased prosperity for the region, it has a hip bellcast roof where the operator's bay extends through the roofline to a hipped roof of its own. Lower extensions on each end also display hip bellcast rooflines while separate eaves extend over the platform. Construction material includes painted stucco above a brick base. Although agent-less, the station remains an overnight stop on VIA Rail's *Ocean Limited*.

Mont-Joli

A large brick station built by the ICR in 1913, it is a highlight of Mont-Joli's downtown. This solid building is distinguished by a large gable on both track and street sides, where semi-circular windows are surrounded with stone keystones and lentils. As with Rimouski, the large station in Mont-Joli reflects the growth of the region.

Levis

The ICR station in Levis began life in 1864 as a town hall and farmers' market. In 1876, when the ICR took over GTR tracks from Rivière-du-Loup to Levis, the market became a station. Built of stone, the two-storey station boasts few architectural embellishments and is simple in style, with a hip roof punctuated by small dormers. Now renovated inside, and with tracks gone since 1993, the historic building is a terminal for buses and for the ferry that crosses the St. Lawrence to

Quebec City. Although trackless, the platform canopy remains in place.

THE STATIONS OF THE GASPÉ

Port-Daniel

Until deteriorating track conditions put at a least a temporary end to train travel, VIA Rail's Gaspé train oceanside route was among its most scenic. Several historic stations survive along this line. The one at Port-Daniel overlooks the ocean. Built in 1908 by the Atlantic Quebec and Western Railway, it displays a simple plan, being one storey with hip gables and overhanging eave. Much of the wood exterior and many interior features remain unaltered. There are bay windows on three sides, including the end of the waiting room. The station served as the rail line's Gaspé terminal until a tunnel through the rocky headland could be completed. The attractive LeGrand Hotel, with its mansard roof, looms nearby.

VIA's Port-Daniel station is one of many historic stations which line the Gaspé Peninsula.

Several other stations survive along this line, many similar in style to that in Port-Daniel. These include Chandler, Bonaventure, Caplan, and Percé (although the station at Percé is located well inland from the famous rock of the same name). The intriguing station at Barachois, while affording a grand view over the ocean, is distinctive in style with a sweeping bellcast roofline. Tracks end at the village of Gaspé, where the CNR's postwar flat-roofed style of station, brick on a stone foundation, awaits travellers.

New Carlisle

Also located on VIA's scenic Gaspé route, this two-storey wooden station was added by the CNR in 1947 to serve its busy yards in this location. New Carlisle may be the last survivor of a style used by the CNR in many areas of eastern Quebec. While the white wooden building remains in good condition, the yards are empty and most of the remaining tracks overgrown.

Matapédia

Situated near the mouth of the Matapédia River, this ICR station was built in 1903 using the company's common pattern: a hip-gable roof with a hip-gable dormer. The wooden structure includes a 1950s extension. It is here that the rail line splits, with a portion veering toward Halifax, while the other makes its way along the Gaspé Peninsula.

Amqui

Situated along the Matapédia River north of the rail junction station at Matapédia, the two-storey wooden station in the village of Amqui was built in 1904 by the ICR. It does not conform to the ICR's standard plans, with its full second floor for the agent and family. The hip gables offer three dormers. The station is now a restaurant, La Vieille Gare; VIA passengers travelling on the *Ocean Limited* now must wait in a heated shelter.

The nearby ICR station at Sayabec similarly no longer functions as a station. Its style is more typical of the ICR, however, with a single-storey hip-gable roof and a small hip dormer above the operator's bay window. Further north along the track VIA may stop at the Causapscal station, a simple, low, single-storey structure with a small dormer in the bellcast roofline.

QUEBEC'S NORTH SHORE STATIONS

Gare du Palais

The fantastic Gare du Palais in Quebec City resembles a fairy-tale palace. It is the finest example of a purely Chateau-style station in Canada (Vancouver's second CPR station looked similar, but lasted only a few years). The Palais station complements not only the Fairmont Le Chateau Frontenac, which rises high above, but the whole ambience of this ancient walled city. Designed by the CPR team of architects led by Harry Pringle, the station opened in 1915 and was, at the time, the only "union" station in the province. It is located in the lower town near the harbour and adjacent to the equally magnificent Chateau-style post office.

This castle is marked with a steep copper roof bracketed by two high conical towers beside a soaring bay that

Architecturally and aesthetically, VIA's Gare du Palais in Quebec City is the grandest in eastern Canada.

rises the full height of the building. The coats of arms of seven prominent Canadians — including General James Wolfe, General Louis-Joseph de Montcalm, Governor Charles de Montmagny, and le Comte de Frontenac — are inserted in the glass panes. Constructed of brick with limestone highlights, the soaring great hall inside consists of separate waiting rooms for men and women (a rule no longer enforced), and an elaborately adorned vaulted ceiling and mezzanine.

Much history lingers inside with the preserved former ticket counters of the CNR and Quebec Central Railway. Visitors can grasp the brass railings on the mezzanine level and view the activity from the second floor. However, little of that activity relates to the railway, as most of the interior has been given over to bars and restaurants. Outside, the station can be viewed nicely from a large landscaped park across the street. The building is on Rue de la Gare du Palais.

The interior of the Gare du Palais offers a display of decorative grandeur.

Trois-Rivières

This Beaux-Arts station was built in 1925 and designed by the firm of Ross and MacDonald, who also designed Toronto's grand Union Station. The stone station in Trois-Rivières is the largest along the CPR between Quebec City and Montreal. With its flat roof and subdued design features, at the time it represented a new era in station styles. Although two storeys in the centre, a single storey extends around the perimeter. A series of pillars mark the small entranceway. Inside the high-ceilinged waiting room, a traditional clock and a series of railway themed murals by famed muralist Adam Sheriff Scott are featured. The train sheds can still be seen by the tracks, although passenger service ended with the "great VIA massacre" in 1990. The building now serves as a bus terminal.

L'Epiphanie

Up until 1990 VIA Rail operated a service along the CPR's north shore line between Quebec City and Montreal. Many early stations, especially those constructed in the 1880s by the Quebec, Montreal, Ottawa and Occidental Railway (QMO&O), remained as VIA waiting rooms. These stood at Pont-Rouge, Berthier, La Chevrotière, Lanoraie, Saint-Basile, and Sainte-Anne-de-la-Pérade.

The one-time CPR station in L'Épiphanie, Quebec, has remained closed since VIA Rail was forced to end service in 1990. It is the last of its kind.

The station in L'Epiphanie was built in 1923 to replace an older structure. Designated under the HRSPA, it is one of only two rural stations to survive on the north shore route. With no apparent local interest in repurposing the building, it sits vacant. Being situated apart from the village itself, no other railway related structure is to be seen.

Sainte-Anne-de-la-Pérade

Sadly, the Sainte-Anne-de-la-Pérade station is the last surviving original QMO&O station built in 1877 along what is now the CPR line between Quebec and Montreal. The style is unlike any others in Canada. The wide roof extends over the platform, but also beyond the end gables. Distinctive, too, is the steep cross gable over the operator's bay with extended eaves. In 2014 the structure was restored as a private residence. The station was designated under the HRSPA in 1992. An identical station in Sainte-Geneviève-de-Berthier was likewise designated, but neglect made restoring it impossible, so it was demolished.

Lachute

Built in 1929 to replace an earlier QMO&O wooden station, this station uses the same plans as many others, namely Shawiniga. The building is made from brick with stone trim on the corners and around the windows and doors. It is set off with a high cross gable and bell-cast, hip roof. Located near the centre of the busy downtown, it now serves as tourist information and economic development offices. The once-busy yards are now quiet and bereft of other railway structures.

Closer to Ottawa on the old QMO&O line is one of the few surviving QMO&O stations. The wooden Masson station was erected in 1877, and sports the typical high cross gable with gable ends and wide eaves. Although designated under the HRSPA, it remains boarded up. Such is the case too with the Calumet QMO&O station between Masson and Lachute. It follows the same pattern as that at Masson, and is similarly boarded up.

Joliette

The Great Northern Railway was a relatively short-lived line that received a charter to build a route from Quebec to Ottawa, passing north of Montreal. Its station at Joliette, built in 1901, is the last GNR-built station to survive. In 1910 the CNoR (known in Quebec as the Canadian Northern Quebec Railway), assumed control of the line and created a divisional point at Joliette.

The station is unique. Resembling the distinctive hip-gable masterpieces that Joseph Hobson created for the Great Western Railway in Ontario, this two-storey brick station displays hip cross gables at each end with dormers between. Although unstaffed, it still serves VIA customers travelling on its wilderness routes to Jonquière and Senneterre.

Shawinigan

This industrial city on the Saint-Maurice River enjoys two nearly identical, designated railway stations. The one built by the CPR in 1927 is a storey-and-a-half, brick-on-stone building that features a prominent cross gable that rises above the operator's bay, with its triple windows and imitation stone accents around the windows and on the corners. The roof is bellcast. The building is situated well away from the centre of the town in a largely industrial area.

The station built by CNR is closer to the commercial core of Shawinigan. Built two years after the CPR station, it replicates its rival's style in nearly every aspect. It, too, sports a distinctive high cross gable above the operator's bay with the original town name, "Shawinigan Falls," as well as stone trim around the windows and the corners. In an effort to attract the tourist trade, the station also contained a restaurant. While it remains a shelter for VIA Rail trains travelling to Jonquière and Senneterre, the ticket agent has been removed and although restoration work is under way, the building is only open for waiting train passengers.

QUEBEC'S NORTHERN STATIONS

Stations of Le P'tit Train du Nord

The Northern Colonization Railway, a CPR subsidiary, was one of several lines built to help colonize the Laurentian area of northern Quebec. The route led northwesterly from Montreal's Jean-Talon station, making its way into the looming Laurentian Mountains. While the initial purpose was settlement, by the 1920s, skiing was enjoying a boom in popularity, and the potential of the Laurentians to attract aficionados of the sport was not lost on the CPR.

Most of the original stations sported the QMO&O designs with wide steeply gables roofs. Later

replacements were drawn strictly from the CPR book of station patterns.

Several stations along that line have been preserved or replicated. The initiative began in the town of L'Annonciation when the CPR threatened to remove the wooden station. It was built in 1903 to a standard CPR plan, known as Plan No. 4 — a single-storey building with a wide roof and extended, wraparound eaves. It was perhaps the most commonly used CPR plan in Canada. The local initiative to save the building resounded throughout the area resulting in one of Canada's most extensive station-saving initiatives.

The station at nearby Nominingue is in the same style. Both, repainted in the original yellow and red colours, serve as tourist offices. Labelle and Mont-Rolland each host two-storey stations preserved along the line. Labelle was named in honour of Father Antoine Labelle, the parish priest who initiated the colonization movement into the area. The

The former QMO&O station in Saint Jovite, Quebec, is a well-preserved example of the distinctive stations the company built along the route of Le P'tit Train du Nord in the Laurentians.

Mont-Rolland station is built with wood siding and houses a restaurant and information centre. A caboose and baggage cart on the grounds help enhance the heritage of the building. The latter houses a bicycle rental shop.

The Saint-Jovite, Prévost, and Piedmont stations display features of the original QMO&O-style stations on the line, with steep gables above the operator's bay and steep extended end gables. The latter two remain on-site on the bike trail. Saint-Jovite's original station was moved to the busy main street of the town to become a restaurant. To enhance the railway theme, the exterior has been restored, and tracks put in place along the front of the station.

The Sainte-Agathe-des-Monts station, with its distinctive witch's hat roof over the waiting room, was designated under the HRSPA, but, sadly, burned beyond repair in 2008. Undeterred, the town rebuilt most of the structure to its original appearance and it now houses a tourist office and meeting facilities.

Following a devastating fire in the Sainte-Agathe-des-Monts station, the community rallied to replicate the unusual structure.

The station in Mont-Laurier was built in 1909 and marks the northern terminus of the rail line and of the rail trail. It was built using one of the CPR's standard plans found in many parts of Ontario and across the Prairies. Its two-storey central block displays a pair of hip dormers in the roofline surmounting two windows each. Single wings stretch out from each end, although no other railway features remain. The station now houses the Café de la Gare bar and restaurant.

The original southern end of the bike trail lies at the handsome station in Saint-Jérôme. (The trail has since been extended to Blainville closer to Montreal.) Now a growing suburb of Montreal, the town has saved the station, which was federally designated in 1994, and created around it a plaza with fountains and a caboose display. The station was built in 1897 to a grander CPR plan with a rough stone exterior above a stone base. This Richardsonian-style building displays the wide arched windows and openings typical of that architectural style, as well as a pronounced bellcast roof.

BEYOND THE LAURENTIANS

Trains today follow one of two routes from Montreal into the Laurentians. Following the route of the CNoR from Montreal , the tracks lead to Hervey-Jonction where the line splits, one aiming northeast to Jonquière, the other northwest to Senneterre. The latter is but a stub of the once mighty National Transcontinental Railway.

The NTR was Prime Minister Wilfred Laurier's plan to build a second transcontinental railway across

Canada. His NTR would, along with the Grand Trunk Western as a partner, link Moncton with Vancouver. Because of his haste to build the line from Moncton to Prince Rupert, the many way stations used an almost identical pattern — storey-and-a-half with hip-gable roofs and hip dormers above the operator's bay, and sometimes on the ends if a larger structure was needed. The station at still found in Macamic in the Abitibi region of Quebec is an example of the most common design. Built in 1910, it is a one-and-half-storey wooden building with a hip dormer in the steep roof representing the agent's apartment. Now a town hall, much of the interior has been altered although the exterior retains its original appearance. A similar pattern also remains in the remote community of Clova along the Montreal to Senneterre rail line. It still functions as a VIA Rail station stop and is designated under the HRSPA.

Now a municipal office, the NTR station in Macamic, Quebec, is built in a style that is repeated by hundreds of other stations on the cross-Canada route.

Senneterre

The NTR placed divisional points at Fitzpatrick, Parent, and Senneterre. Senneterre, at first, had a station that used a pattern more commonly found in the NTR's rural stations, similar to that at Macamic. When the Senneterre was chosen for a divisional point, the station was doubled in size. When it burned in 1953 the CNR constructed an International-style brick structure with a typical flat roof. Two storeys in height, the second floor housed the various railway offices needed in such a location. The waiting room currently has been reduced in area, and many of the office functions no longer exist. However, the station remains the terminus of the Montreal–Senneterre VIA Rail train known as the *Abitibi*, popular with hunters, fishers, and trappers, and essential to First Nations residents.

Other stations of note along the Senneterre route include the two-storey wooden station at Hervey-Jonction, and the station at La Tuque. At Hervey-Jonction the trains to Jonquiere (*Saguenay*) and Senneterre respectively split to their destinations.

Val-d'Or

In the 1930s the CNR extended a branch line from Senneterre to the burgeoning mining towns of Val-d'Or and Rouyn-Noranda. Here, the company adopted a different style of station: a large two-storey structure with hip gables at each end. It placed similar stations in Noranda, Cadillac, and Malartic. While the latter three were removed in the 1990s and early 2000s, the station in Val d'Or, built in 1937, was bought by the town and now serves as a food bank. In the 1920s the Ontario

Northland Railway extended a branch from Swastika on its main line into the mining region where it erected a single-storey brick building which now functions as home for the Projet St. Michel. The tracks adjacent to the platform have been relocated.

After splitting from the Abitibi at Hervey-Jonction en route to Jonquiere, the *Saguenay* passes eastern Canada's last active CNoR station in Lac-Édouard, with its trademark pyramid roof, a speciality of CNoR architect R.B. Pratt.

Hebértville

As the *Saguenay* begins its descent toward Lac-Saint-Jean, it stops at Hébertville. The 1933 CN station there was built to replace an earlier building destroyed by fire, and displays a standard CNR plan with a simple hip roof. An Arts and Crafts–style of building, it exhibits bay windows on both the track and street sides. Windows and doors are multi-paned with transoms, while the door is flanked by cottage-like sash windows. Although the location remains a station stop, it no longer offers the service of an agent.

Built in the postwar International style, the flat-roofed station at once-busy Chambord Junction, the next stop on the Jonquiere line, retains both a VIA Rail waiting room and CNR functions. The new station in Jonquiere itself is a modern building, which serves both as a bus station and VIA stop. The handsome brick station in Arvida, east of Jonquiere, is no longer a station stop; it is now a funeral home. Built of brick on concrete, the extended station contains split-level hip bellcast roofs and a hip canopy above the street-side entrance. Following its closure in the 1980s it had served as a tavern.

Although trains no longer travel that far, the 1920 grand two-storey brick-and-stone former terminal in Chicoutimi is marked by a pair of hip gables on what was the track side. Since VIA vacated the building in 1987, it has been considerably expanded and repurposed as a shopping centre and office building. Even its original size reflected its role not only as one-time railway terminal, but as a port of entry for ships that have travelled up the Saguenay River from the St. Lawrence carrying passengers or freight.

Témiscaming

Originally known as Long Sault, this site began as a key stopping place for Ottawa River steamships. In 1887 a narrow-gauge tramway was extended along the shores of the Ottawa River. In 1888 Alex Lumsden opened a sawmill on Gordon Creek, and three years later the CPR acquired the line, adding a wooden station on the Ottawa River. In 1918 when the Riordan Pulp and Paper Company opened its mills, it hired Scottish architect Thomas Adams to lay out a new town based on the "garden city" movement. Curving streets, central parks, and Arts and Crafts–style houses and apartments appeared.

As did a new station. Designed by New Brunswick architect Jasper Humphrey, it was completed in 1927, with accommodation for the agent and his family on the second floor marked by two hip gables. This new urban station boasted a high-ceiling waiting room with arched doorways between the waiting rooms. The street entrance, with its high, two-storey gable, stands prominently at the end of a treed avenue which crosses the bridge over Gordon River. Following a fire in 1994, the

Built as part of the Garden City movement, the former CPR station in Témiscaming, Quebec, now houses the Musée de la Gare.

citizens fought off attempts to demolish the building and created a museum in the station. The station received heritage status in 1997.

La Musée de la Gare displays much of the line's history (it was known as the Mocassin Line) and early images of the town's history as well as a photo collection of stations that appeared along the line from Témiscaming to Angliers. That at Témiscaming is the only surviving station anywhere on the line.

THE STATIONS OF NOVA SCOTIA

The dominant station builders in Nova Scotia were the ICR, which later became part the Canadian National Railway; the CNoR, which was assembled by the railway building duo of William Mackenzie and Donald Mann; and the CPR's Dominion Atlantic Railway. The ICR, in particular, created a number of spectacular station styles, a good number of which remain on site and preserved.

The CPR, however, tended to rely upon its book of station patterns, leaving few to celebrate. The CNoR stuck to its usual pyramid roof plans which they used from coast to coast. In total, about forty stations have lingered in the province, many of which still stand on their original sites.

Pictou

The ICR, built in the 1870s to link Canada's eastern provinces, created some of the region's finest stations, a few of which are still around. The 1901 Pictou terminal station was one of the line's finest. This grand two-storey brick station, which faces the Northumberland Strait, is an extensive structure with three high-peaked cross gables on its roof. Detailing such as the arched and Palladian windows on the second floor, which served as offices for ICR employees, set the station apart. It earlier served as the terminal for rail cars being ferried to Prince Edward Island (which now operates from nearby Caribou to Woods Island,

Noted for its grand station architecture, the Intercolonial Railway created this stunning — and still active — station in Amherst, Nova Scotia.

PEI). Passenger service ended in 1963, and the tracks have since been lifted. Despite a fire in 1996, the building now houses a fishermen's museum and other community services. Previously, in 1976, the federal government declared the Pictou station a National Historic Site.

Amherst

Here lies another one of eastern Canada's most attractive ICR railway stations and one of Nova Scotia's largest. Built by the ICR in 1908, it displays the Romanesque Revival style with full two-storey bay windows on both track and street side. Its building material is a warm red sandstone quarried locally. The roofline rises above the second storey to a pyramid, while many of its graceful arched windows and doorways are tripartite in style. VIA Rail still boards passengers here on its Atlantic service. It has been designated under the HRSPA.

Sackville

A close neighbour of Amherst is the sandstone station in Sackville, New Brunswick. One and a half storeys, it was one of the last to be built by the ICR and was completed in 1908. It lies some distance from the centre of the community and overlooks the Tantramar Marshes. Its wraparound bellcast roof extends over the station platform while a large gabled dormer rest above the operator's bay window. Few railway related buildings remain in the area. Designated under the HRSPA, the station remains a stop for VIA Rail's Halifax to Montreal *Ocean Limited* train.

Tatamagouche

The ICR stations in Tatamagouche and Pugwash are very similar in style. Both were built on ICR branch lines in 1886 and 1890, respectively, and were said to be designed by Sandford Fleming himself. These brick structures rise two storeys, with steep rooflines and bay windows that rise into a prominent cross gable, while equally steep gables mark the ends of the roof. The stations contained separate doors to the gender-specific waiting rooms at the ends of the building, and had a freight shed extension on the end.

In 1974 eighteen-year-old James Lefresne bought the vacant Tatamagouche building, saving it from demolition, although thirteen years would pass before restoration began. Two years later it opened as the Train Station Inn. The last train to Tatamagouche departed in 1986 (and ended up stuck in snow). The Tatamagouche Station Inn with coaches and cabooses serving as accommodation and a restaurant, opened in 1989, while the station in Pugwash now houses a public library.

Antigonish

Reminiscent of the Amherst station, the lovely brick ICR station in Antigonish was built in 1908. It was designed by William Mackenzie, the ICR's chief engineer in Moncton, and the likely architect of the line's other grand stations at Moncton, Rivière-du-Loup (both since replaced), and Amherst. The brick-on-stone building features steep rooflines with a prominent cross gable, which itself contains small dormers. The sweeping bellcast hip gables also contain small dormers. Passenger service no longer exists, and the structure now houses the Antigonish Heritage Museum.

Halifax

Built in 1927 by the CNR, the neoclassical station in Halifax replaced the ICR station destroyed in the Halifax explosion of 1917. The entrance is through a series of pillars into a large, high-ceilinged waiting room with an open steel roof truss work and skylights. Interior features include original light fixtures, a bronze display cabinet, and terrazzo floors. Built of limestone, the style is known as Beaux-Arts, a common trend in the 1920s and 1930s. With its adjoining Nova Scotian Hotel, it was the last combined station/hotel built in Canada.

On the main line northwest of Halifax, the 1923 CNR station in Elmsdale is to be the new home of the Nova Scotia Railway Heritage Society.

Orangedale

The wooden ICR station at Orangedale is the sole survivor of an attractive station plan developed by the ICR and used across northern Nova Scotia and Cape Breton Island in the 1880s. The station was constructed in 1886, with trains arriving five years later. The station rises two storeys, with four dormers set into the steep roof on the front, including a prominent cross gable above the operator's bay. The roofline in the centre rises further to a pyramid shape.

While the main level provided waiting rooms and a ticket office, the second floor provided accommodation for the agent and his family. Historically, the station was the most important between Canso and Sydney. Passenger service ended in the 1990s. The station is celebrated as a museum with a railway display, as well as in the melodic and ironically appropriate lament by the songwriting Rankin Family, "The Orangedale Whistle."

Louisburg

This interesting station is somewhat of an anomaly in Nova Scotia. It was built in 1895 by the Sydney and Louisburg Railway, which transported coal from the coal mines at Sydney to waiting ships. Its style is unusual in that the steep roof contains steeply pitched twin gables on the street side with equally steep gables at each end. The wooden structure offers a wide wraparound canopy. The line was busy with thirty-one steam locomotives operating on only 187 kilometres of track. In fact, the line operated with steam until 1966. The station closed in 1968 and the tracks were removed. Thanks to the efforts of past employees, local enthusiasts, and local government, the station was saved and opened as a museum in 1972. A freight shed has also survived and coaches stand on the tracks in front of historic building.

Sydney Mines and North Sydney

Meanwhile, Sydney Mines has itself retained its 1904 ICR station. It lacks the imaginative flair of other ICR stations, using instead a fairly simple and common standard plan. It is a single storey, made of brick, with a hip dormer above the operator's bay. The station was closed in 1990 and is now the Sydney Mines Heritage Museum and Cape Breton Fossil Centre. North Sydney, too, has managed to hang onto not one, but two stations. The more recent of the two was built in to a standard plan in 1916, with a single storey and a hip roof with a small dormer above the operator's bay.

But the original 1880s ICR station stands a short distance away and is a much grander two-storey station with a high mansard roof, a cross-gable tower that rises above the operator's bay, which is flanked by a pair of dormers, and includes an arched dormer of its own. The platform has been since enclosed to form a porch in addition to other extensions. The brick building is now painted a brilliant white and, after serving as a lumber office, remains in private use. It lies across the street from the more recent station.

Also on Cape Breton Island, a branch of the ICR was the Inverness Railway where the Inverness station is now a museum, while the Port Hood station serves as a funeral home.

The Canadian Northern in Nova Scotia

It was the plan of William Mackenzie and Donald Mann to cobble together a Trans-Canada rail network, and to this end they added to their growing empire the Halifax and Southwestern Railway, a line from Halifax to Yarmouth. The stations reflect the standard CNoR plans used primarily across the Prairies. The larger stations consisted of the iconic two-storey pyramid roof with single-storey extensions at each end. These were most commonly constructed at divisional points and in larger communities. All featured hip or peaked dormers in the main roof and extensions. Examples of these survive in Chester (a tourist office) and Liverpool (the Hank Snow Home Town Museum).

The company's more common plan for smaller towns and villages, known as their Class 3 plan, was a single block with a two-storey pyramid roof and single-storey extension at one end to serve as a freight shed. Although many were built along the line, the one surviving example of this style in Nova Scotia is situated in French River Village in Upper Tantallon. It now contains a bike rental shop for the cycling trail on the former roadbed and small café for hungry trail users. Another example of this style is now a museum in Musquodoboit Harbour, situated to the northeast of Halifax, although it was in fact built by the Canadian National Railway shortly after it assumed the bankrupt CNoR. The village of Hubbards enjoys a replica of its CNoR Class 3 station, which reopened in 2002 as an information centre. The original station was removed in 1977.

In the UNESCO heritage town of Lunenburg, the Tudoresque CNR station is all but forgotten. It was built in 1923 and displays three cross gables on

The iconic pyramid roof on the former station in French River Village, Nova Scotia, confirms that it was a typical Canadian Northern Railway station, a pattern the upstart line repeated across the country.

a storey-and-a-half structure. Following the closure of the railway spur line into the town it became a police station and now houses the offices of the South Shore Tourist Association.

THE STATIONS OF THE DOMINION ATLANTIC RAILWAY

Hantsport

This one-storey brick station was, in fact, built by the CPR in 1943, long after its acquisition of the DAR. The style harkens back to more traditional station designs, with a central gable rising from the operator's bay into the roofline. Hantsport is clearly an industrial town, to which the station is more orientated than to the residential or commercial areas. The building is a designated station under the HRSPA.

Annapolis Royal

By 1915 the CPR was leasing the DAR and designing its new stations. The one at Annapolis Royal incorporated a common CPR style. Under its wide, low hip roof were wraparound eaves that extended over the platform. Unlike most stations along the DAR line, which were constructed of wood, the Annapolis Royal station used brick on a concrete base. In order to attract tourists to local attractions, the CPR incorporated arched windows and doors with transoms beside and above the openings. Its slate roof was set off with a copper roll. Passenger service ended in 1990 and the tracks were removed. Today the building houses the Clean Annapolis River Project. It was designated under the HRSPA in 1992.

Wolfeville

After the now demolished station in Kentville, the Wolfeville DAR station was one of the largest on the line. Built of brick in 1912, it was designed by Herbert Gates, with the agent's quarters on the second level. Basic in style, the station consists of a hip roof atop a two-storey block. In 1991 the Wolfeville Memorial Library Fund raised $275,000 to convert the treasured building into a library. Renovated in 1993 by Rhodes, Curry and Co., it received the Nova Scotia Heritage Trust Award. Besides books and DVDs, the library contains a scale model of Locomotive No. 32, known as the *Bloomington*, which had been built in 1908, as well as a model of the observation car the *Annapolis Royal*.

At the end of the line in Yarmouth, which formerly contained stations from both the DAR and the Halifax and Southwestern (later the CNoR), the local Tim Hortons on Water Street, next to the site of the DAR station, has celebrated the town's railway roots by designing its outlet to be a replica of the DAR's first station.

Other DAR stations to survive the demise of the rail line include those at Billtown, relocated to become a workshop with its exterior restored; the 1919 Tudor Revival brick station at Bridgetown, which is now the End of the Line Pub; the postwar two-storey, flat-roofed Cornwallis station, now a garage; and the 1928 Kingston station, relocated near to its original spot and converted into a fire hall.

One of the better preservation efforts is that undertaken at Middleton, where the 1915 standard single-storey wooden chalet-style CPR station built in 1915 has been restored as the Middleton Railway Museum.

THE STATIONS OF NEW BRUNSWICK

New Brunswick had a great variety of station styles due the remarkable number of different lines that operated in the province, some even before it was a province. Nearly three dozen remain in various uses, most of which have remained on their original sites.

Sussex

In 1859 the New Brunswick Railway took over the European and North American Railway and completed its line from Saint John to Shediac, giving the community of Sussex, located midway, an economic boost. In 1913 the then-new owner of the line, the Intercolonial Railway, showed why it was a leading builder of grand stations by adding a Queen Anne–style brick centrepiece to the town. One and a half storeys high and constructed of brick with stone trim,

The ticket windows are but part of the excellent preservation effort of the Intercolonial station in Sussex, New Brunswick.

the structure displays prominent gables on both the track and street sides. The main entrance includes a dormer above a parapet, while the roofline consists of multiple hip gables. A covered walkway links the station to the freight shed. The building now houses a museum and tourist office and is well preserved.

Sadly, the town has chosen to place an unattractive chain link fence along the tracks. While safety is important, a wrought iron fence would have been more attractive and appropriate for such a magnificent structure. The station was designated under the HRSPA in 1995 and is listed on the Canadian Registry of Heritage Properties.

Hampton

This modest station, simple in style as was the CNR's wont, was added to the landscape of this small village in 1922 and served as a station until 1974. The town's railway history dates to 1859, with the completion of the New Brunswick Railway (originally the E&NA) from Saint John to Shediac. A short-lived branch led to St. Martins on the sea, but its days ended in 1940. Bay windows on both sides of the structure attest to this dual role. The building is a single storey, with a wide sloping hip roof. The interior remains well preserved, and today contains a gift shop and tourist information.

Rothesay

The former station near the Saint John suburb of Rothesay is a rare surviving example of the standard style used by one the Maritimes' first railways, the European and North American Railway. Many of

Still around after all these years is Canada's oldest station, the European and North American Railway station built at Rothesay, New Brunswick, in 1854.

Canada's first stations more closely resembled stage coach stops, with a simple two-storey construction. Built in 1858 in a neo-gothic style, the two-and-a-half storey building retains many original exterior features, including a wraparound eave. Still on its original site, the station was declared a National Historic Site in 1976 and is now a private residence.

Shediac

The European and North American Railway from Saint John to Pointe-du-Chêne (now Shediac) was one of the first lines built in the province in 1858. The Shediac station, however, dates from 1901, and was designed by Acadian architect Alfred Sincennes in what is called the Craftsman style. Like many other Maritime stations, it is a single-storey structure with a noticeable hip dormer above the operator's bay window. Constructed of stone, it now serves as a municipal building, the tracks long gone.

Rogersville

Built by the CNR in 1930, the Rogersville VIA station, although not designated, is the last operating rural heritage station in New Brunswick. It is single storey with a wide bellcast roof that extends over the platform, but is distinguished by a hip gable bay entrance on the street side.

THE CPR IN NEW BRUNSWICK

One of eastern Canada's earliest railway lines was the New Brunswick and Canada Railway from St. Andrews to Woodstock. Later CPR extensions included links to Fredericton and Edmunston and eventually a main line from Montreal through Maine to Saint John, a route known as the Short Line.

Aroostook

This small community on the Saint John River served as a junction between the NBR and the Aroostook Valley Railway. After it purchased the lines, the CPR chose Aroostook as a new divisional point and added housing, a roundhouse, and a small station. Although modest in scale, the wooden station includes a small dormer perched on a steep bellcast roof with hip gables on the ends. Although designated as a protected station under the HRSPA, it sits neglected and overgrown. While all other railway buildings are gone, their sites obliterated by bush, the rail bed now forms part of the Trans-Canada Trail.

Grand Falls

The tracks of the CPR's NBR lines also lead past the bustling mill town of Grand Falls where, on the south end of town, the CPR added a small wooden station similar to that in Arroostook. A hip gable marks one end of the structure, a peaked gable the other end. There is a second station in in Grand Falls that dates to the building of the NTR from Moncton to the West Coast. The building rises two storeys, with an interesting hip-gable roof. Extensions to each side of the central section are of a single storey with bellcast rooflines. Unusual, too, in that the building has retained its wood construction with ship-slab siding below the window line and wood shingles above. Built in 1912 to a standard, but rarely used NTR plan, the station it the last of its kind. As with the Grand Falls CPR station, this building lies in an industrial area and is nowhere near the main part of the town. Designated under the HRSPA, it sits vacant awaiting reuse.

Florenceville

The former CPR station at Florenceville now sits on the roadbed of the CPR line in Bristol, looking not at all out of place, especially since the original Bristol station was identical in style. Built of wood in the CPR's Chalet style, the small station has been immaculately restored. It was relocated to this spot in 2000 by the Shogomoc Rail Club. Outside the station, there are three classic CPR coaches which are now a fine dining restaurant.

Burtts Corner

Few stations were built using this plan, and the one at Burtts Corner northwest of Fredericton is the last of its kind (another in Bath has been heavily altered). A gangly wooden affair, it stands a full two storeys in height with small cross-gables at each end of the roof. Much of the exterior remains little altered. Now in private hands, it is a designated heritage station.

Edmunston

Although part of the CPR's plan to link Saint John, New Brunswick, with the St. Lawrence Valley, the New Brunswick Railway originally never extended beyond Edmunston. Completed in 1929, replacing a station destroyed by fire, this single-storey brick station with an unadorned hip roof is simple in style, as the CPR was moving away from the elaborate stations of its earlier era. Richardsonian in influence, the operator's bay is adorned with a double pair of arched windows as is the main entranceway. Designated under the HRSPA in 1991, the station's interior has been little altered and includes gendered waiting rooms and the agent's ticket office. The Irving Company donated the property to Edmunston in 1998. The city restored the station and in 2007 opened it as a tourism centre.

A second station in Edmunston dates to 1959, though rail service to the town began with the building of the NTR in 1912. This CNR station, designated under the HRSPA, was built to the International style of the CNR's postwar stations. The sleek, flat-roofed station is similar to the one in Senneterre in northern Quebec. Two storeys in height, it also sports a three-storey tower. The extensive structure contained offices on the second floor, although the former waiting rooms and ticket office on the main floor were closed when passenger service here halted in the 1980s. Following the CN's departure from the building, an unsympathetic new third-floor addition has compromised some of the very features for which it was designated.

Fredericton

In 1923 the CPR constructed a new brick station to serve the province's capital city. Replacing an earlier wooden structure, this two-storey station displays a rare tapestry brick pattern. The main building is topped by a medium hip roof, while two wings are one and one-and-a-half storeys with gable roofs. The building marked the original terminus of the CPR's Fredericton Branch Line from Saint John. After years of neglect and controversy, the

building has been extensively renovated and enlarged and is now part of a liquor store. It also serves as a meeting hall and event venue. The roadbed forms part of a walking trail.

McAdam, New Brunswick's Heritage Treasure

One of the few stations in Canada to be declared a National Historic Site, the massive Chateauesque stone pile in the once-remote railway junction of McAdam, New Brunswick, is probably the most visually stunning of eastern Canada's stations. It was designed by the CPR's go-to architects Edward Maxwell and W.S. Painter and was opened in 1901, replacing a much smaller station (now a residence elsewhere in the town). Additions were added later. The site marked the junction between the earlier New Brunswick Railway (St. Andrews to Woodstock) and the CPR's east coast Short Line from

Following years of debate, the one-time CPR station in Fredericton, New Brunswick, has been repurposed as a meeting venue and liquor store.

One of the most surprising sights in the small New Brunswick community of McAdam is the Maritime's most stunning station, incorporating a second-floor hotel to accommodate vacationers bound for the Algonquin Resort in St. Andrews by-the-Sea.

Montreal to Saint John. As the CPR grew busier and the bucolic Algonquin Inn in St. Andrews grew more popular, the CPR decided on a new station.

But not just any new station.

Maxwell and Painter were to design something special, and that was a three-storey granite Chateau-style station that would outclass any station that Maritime Canada had to offer. Made of grey granite with red granite highlights, the building features a lofty pyramid roof and a prominent hip cross gable at one end. Puncturing the roofline a string of peaked gable dormers mark the seventeen hotel rooms. Staff either boarded in town or found accommodation on the third floor.

On the ground floor were the elaborate separate waiting rooms for ladies and gents, including toilets, as well as a dining room and the hotel lobby. A comfortable sitting room was named the Maxwell Room after the chief architect of the building. Other obvious functions

One of the McAdam station's features was its first class hotel. The lobby is decorated with wood trim and known as the Maxwell Room, named for its architect.

included freight operations, maintenance crew, and a one-cell jail. Tracks run on both sides of the building.

Restored by the town, with aid from federal and provincial grants and dedicated volunteers, the station is more than a museum. The dining room is available for functions, and the more recent diner with stools and curving counter offers coffee and, at designated times, the station's iconic "Railway Pie," similar to Boston cream pie.

The station saw its last passenger train in 1994 when VIA Rail ended its service on the Montreal to Saint John line. Although the building became a National Historic Site in 1976, twenty years would pass before it opened its doors as a museum. The Irving Company had bought the line from the CPR and donated the station to the town.

Since that time the McAdam Historical Restoration Commission has been restoring the station's original rooms, the most recent being the newsstand, the baggage room, and the express room. Because of its proximity to the U.S. border, a customs room checked arriving cross-border travellers. The Irving family owns heritage coaches in Saint John and twice yearly run a UNICEF tour train to the village. But McAdam is more than just its station as much of the town itself retains several historic railway residences (see chapter 4).

St. Stephen

Like many of the border stations in Quebec, the one opposite to Calais, Maine, in St. Stephen, New Brunswick, is a small but distinctive former station. The single-storey station employs a Craftsman style with a flush gable on the front. Its brickwork is stuccoed, although stone trim encircles the windows and doorway. The station sits on a foundation of local granite. The CPR built it in 1929 to replace an earlier New Brunswick and Canada station. Like its Chateauesque CPR predecessor, the building has a steep multi-hip roof. The line leads to McAdam Junction. The last train pulled away in 1969, and since 1971 the building has served as a town library and more recently a tourist information centre. It was added to the Canadian Register of Historic Places in 2008.

PRINCE EDWARD ISLAND'S MANY STATIONS

Prince Edward Island could claim, without exaggeration, a station every four kilometres. More than sixty survived the closing of the line, although only a handful can be found in their original locations.

Alberton

The station in Alberton was built in 1904 and was designed by Charles Chappell. It consists of granite boulders gathered from local farm fields. This station closed in 1973 and now functions as a tourist information centre.

Kensington

The second — and far more elaborate — boulder station is the one in Kensington. Designed by Chappell as well, it consists of a steep elaborately decorate cross gable, Tudoresque woodwork in the end gables, and an

extended overhanging porticos which are supported by stone columns. Passenger service ended in 1969, and the line was abandoned in 1989. Following further restoration in 2006, the one-and-half-storey station now houses the Island Stone Pub. The building was designated as a National Historic Site in 1976 and, like

The boulder station in Kensington, Prince Edward Island, is only one of two in the province displaying this construction technique.

the station in Alberton, is listed on the Canadian Inventory of Heritage Properties. Kensington's original wooden two storey 1876 station with its mansard roof was relocated to Imperial St. to serve as the agent's residence when the new station opened. It still stands.

Elmira

This station, the eastern terminus of the PEI Railway, uses a plan repeated in many Island locations where station operators were required. With its wide roof and overhanging eaves, it contains a characteristic hip dormer in the roofline. Built in 1912, it is now the Elmira Railway Museum. Other surviving stations built to this style include Emerald Junction, now a dwelling; O'Leary, which is now a lunch bar; Cardigan, now the Old Train Station Farmers market; Morell, with its wood shingle siding and now a welcome centre; and Montague, which has been renovated to accommodate a gift shop and information centre. It, too, was a waterside terminal. A replica of the Georgetown station, with a corner tower, is now a restaurant, depicting the extra embellishment that the PEI Railway gave this port facility.

Summerside

The largest station still standing outside of Charlottetown is the one at Summerside. It resembles a later CNR station, two storeys in height, with a large cross gable and half-timber end gable. It is now a regional library. Across the island, several smaller stations, often with no bay windows, have found uses as farm outbuildings or storage.

Charlottetown

Here we have yet another of Canada's finest architectural examples of a city station. This was built by the PEIR in 1907 to replace an earlier, inadequate wooden train shed. Controversy tended to follow the PEIR, with quarrels over location, cost, and political interference. The station was built by E.A. Wallberg of Montreal and rises three storeys, with the third level consisting of a mansard roof. It was constructed of the lovely red sandstone of the island with Nova Scotia limestone trim. The Richardsonian influence can be seen in the rounded window of the main level. While the main floor served the needs of the passengers with waiting rooms and ticket office, the second floor housed railway staff, and the upper level was available for community meetings. CN ended its passenger service in the 1960s and freight service in 1989. The building served as a farmers' market before the province purchased it in 1996 and moved its administrative offices into it. It continues to serve that role.

ON THE ROCK: THE STATIONS OF NEWFOUNDLAND AND LABRADOR

In contrast to Prince Edward Island, a mere seventeen of Newfoundland's railway stations have discovered new life.

The Brigus Branch

Of the hundreds of stations that stood by the tracks of the legendary Newfoundland Railway, the best collection of survivors lie on the Brigus Branch line to Carbonear.

Opened in 1898, the line saw its last train in 1984. Of the eight stations built on the branch, five still stand. Typical of the style is the station at Carbonear. It was built in 1917 to replace on earlier structure, and displays a broad hip overhanging roof, and an operator's bay. Tracks remain in front where a diesel engine is on display.

Three other stations of this style, although smaller, survive. The one at Clarke's Beach remains on site and in good condition, although unused. Another stands on site on a hill above Harbour Grace. Now owned by the Harbour Grace Historical Society, it houses a museum and is the focus of Gordon G. Pike Railway Heritage Museum and Park. The small station at Western Bay, briefly the end of the line, has a nicely preserved exterior and now serves as the office of the North Shore Regional Development Association.

Another earlier style typical of the Newfoundland Railway's first stations can be found at Spaniards Bay and Bay Roberts. These stations more resemble a simple two-storey house, with gable ends and agent's quarters on the second floor and a waiting room and operator's office on the main level. These original buildings date from the construction of the branch line in 1898. They have, however, been altered to serve as a senior's centre and museum respectively.

The Main Line

In addition to the collection of heritage stations on the Brigus Branch, the Main Line too offers several repurposed stations. In Bishops Falls, the more modern, flat-roofed two-storey station now serves as office space; Clarenville, an earlier building with the standard hip roof, now houses the local historical society; the wooden hip-roof station in Deer Lake still provides passenger service, but on buses; the

small hip-roof wooden station in Glenwood, another standard plan, may become a museum; while the smaller hip-roof wooden station in Port Union has, in fact, been turned into a museum.

The railway line's former terminal station at Lewisporte now houses the offices of the Marine Atlantic Company. On the branch line to Bonavista, only the station at Bonavista itself survives. It is close to the harbour and now home to the T.K. Kellway Senior Citizens Group, though it does maintain a display of railway equipment. A short distance away and now boarded up is the former freight building.

By far the most unusual, and oldest, of the stations along the line is at the one at Avondale. It was built prior to 1880 by the Anglo-Newfoundland Telegraph Company as a telegraph repeater station. In 1898 the Reid Newfoundland Railway Company assumed control of the building to serve its passengers. The station's distinctive mansard roof is not found elsewhere among

Avondale's station is Newfoundland's oldest and includes a train display on the iconic Newfoundland narrow-gauge track.

the province's surviving stations. The wooden building was saved and repainted and now serves as an occasionally opened museum. Here, too, a section of the island's iconic narrow-gauge track is still in place and contains a display of railway equipment.

Another significant station is in Whitbourne. This community was formerly a key divisional point and junction, with branch lines leading to Argentia and Carbonear. Now remodelled into a municipal office, this single-storey hip-roof station, a larger example of the standard railway plans, still stands and includes a display of railway equipment.

When the trains moved out, the Railway Coastal Museum moved in to the CNR station in St. John's, Newfoundland.

St. John's

Designed by W.H. Massey, the Reid Newfoundland's Railway terminal, with waiting rooms and company offices, was completed in 1903. It replaced temporary quarters in what was an old fort, Fort William, at the opposite end of the town. Designed using a combination of Second Empire and Chateau styles, the wide stone building rises three and a half storeys to a mansard roof with a prominent gable in its central block. At the ends are a pair of two-and-a-half-storey mansard roof pavilions, each with a prominent central gable. It contains arched and rounded windows. After passenger service ended in 1969, the building served as a bus terminal, and, after the rail line itself closed, it was converted to the Railway Coastal Museum with a display of passenger equipment beside it.

LIFE ON THE LINE: THE RAILWAY TOWNS

Unlike on the Canadian Prairies, where the railways created the towns, in eastern Canada most of the towns were already there. Mill towns, farm hamlets, stage coach stopping places, and ports all largely predated the arrival of the rails. In that sense, Quebec and the Atlantic provinces can claim few pure railway towns. But, to be sure, there are many towns and villages across the region that bear the mark of the railway.

The most distinctive were the divisional towns. It was at these towns, located every 150 kilometres or so, that the railways needed to put in their roundhouses, their employee housing (be they family dwellings or bunkhouses), their offices, and their maintenance facilities. Where the towns were not created from scratch, they bore distinctive characteristics that many maintain to this day. While divisional towns may not be commercial attractions like museums or tour trains, they nonetheless constitute a visible reminder of the railway heritage of eastern Canada.

Less obvious railway towns are the station satellite villages. These communities were located where the railway companies needed to bypass existing towns, usually to obtain cheaper land for their stations. Although not large, these places would usually offer a station, a railway hotel or two, water towers, and occasionally a grain elevator, as well as a handful of homes for the railway workers. For the most part, these villages are no longer clearly distinguishable as the parent town has often sprawled outward to consume them. But here, too, a few maintain their distinctiveness, and form another visible reminder of the region's railway heritage.

RAILWAY TOWNS OF QUEBEC

Charny

When the Grand Trunk Railway made its way along the south shore of the St. Lawrence River, it established a station stop at Chaudière by the falls of the Chaudière River. When the station moved to the east side of the river, the location became the focus for converging rail lines, including a junction from Charny to the riverside terminal of Levis where ferries took passengers to connecting lines in Quebec City on the far shore.

When the Intercolonial Railway took over the section east of Levis from the Grand Trunk, it established a key rail junction and divisional point yard known as the Joffre yard in Charny. Here, the ICR erected a massive railway roundhouse that still stands and is now a national historic site (see chapter 6). The railway laid out the town in the standard grid network of streets containing boarding houses and employee housing. The yard itself contained the usual maintenance shops, offices, and repair facilities. By the 1950s, 70 percent of Charny's workforce was employed by the CNR.

While a newer and larger marshalling yard now operates further east of the original yard, and even though the old railway community has been greatly overwhelmed by Levis's urban development, some of the railway heritage still lingers in old Charny. In a heritage district known as the District des Cheminots (railwaymen), the 1950s CN station (replacing the ICR station, which in turn had replaced the original GTR station) survives, as does the street pattern and several early structures on it. The Rue du Viaduc offers up several examples of railway housing, especially south of the railway bridge, and along the Rue de la Gare many houses display the wooden duplex style. Some of these buildings served as boarding houses. North of the station along the Rue des Églises stand what were once shops and hotels that served the rail workers.

Several of the streets honour their railway roots with names like Triage (yard), Rotunde (roundhouse), Rue de la Gare (Station Street), Rue du Rail, and even Totillard (meaning milk run).

Meanwhile, at the site of Chaudière Junction west of the river, while no early railway structures survive, the original Grand Trunk route of 1856 to Richmond marks the start of the Lotbinière/Bois Francs Rail Trail. Other features at Charny include the Quebec bridge, opened in 1917 and the largest of its kind in the world (see chapter 6) and the Levis station on the river, which continues to ferry passengers across the river (see chapter 3).

Parent

When the NTR made its way through the forests of northwestern Quebec, it cleared the way for the lumber industry. By 1912 Parent was a NTR divisional town, and in 1920 E.B. Eddy opened a lumber depot. The street pattern displayed the usual grid network both north of the station, where most of the businesses are found along the main street, and south of the rail yard, where the housing was situated. The station followed the standard NTR plan of two storeys with a long hip-gable roof with a small dormer in the centre. The yards contained a coaling tower, bunkhouse, and a twelve-stall engine house.

An investigation of the NTR's divisional stations in the early twentieth century revealed that Parent had been overbuilt, having enough capacity to serve 800 kilometres of line when only 190 kilometres was needed. As a result, the station was replaced with today's simple single-storey wooden structure. Today, Parent remains a busy railway town. It is a regular stop for the many hunters, anglers, canoers, and campers who arrive on the VIA Rail train, the *Abitibi*, from Montreal, and the Kruger sawmill. Even today, Parent is not on a highway network and depends largely on the trains.

With its post–Second World War station, Senneterre in northern Quebec remains a busy divisional town on what was originally the National Transcontinental Railway.

Senneterre

Situated on the Nottaway River, Senneterre began life as a trading post. When the NTR railway builders came through the bush in 1911, they first named the site Nottaway. In 1926 a boiler explosion killed five employees in the then-divisional town of Doucet. The railway moved their facilities to Nottaway, which had been renamed Senneterre in 1919. Here, the original standard NTR rural plan station was expanded to accommodate the divisional functions. But when the station burned in 1949, the CNR, then the line's operator, constructed an International-style station with a second-storey, flat roof, and square features (see chapter 3). With the end of steam, many of the yard features disappeared, including the roundhouse, coal tower, and water tower. New shops were constructed in 1958, as well as a new control tower and bunkhouse.

The town's railway roots are evident throughout. The large station dominates the end of the main street, the grid pattern of streets reflects the usual NTR layout, and many of the dwellings display the style of divisional towns. It remains an active railway town as well, with a three-times weekly VIA train pulling in from Montreal in the early evening (the former overnight train was replaced with a saner daylight service several years ago), and daily freights. The number of disembarking passengers may seem small until one realizes that only a few stops earlier the coaches were packed with cottagers, canoeists, fishermen, and trappers.

Freights loaded with lumber or mining products travel into the marshalling yard from the southwest along the line to Rouyn-Noranda and Val-d'Or.

While the second floor of the station now serves as a bunkhouse for the dwindling number of CN employees, both earlier bunkhouses remain. The older of the two now serves as a clubhouse on the golf course, while the larger and more recent is now an apartment building on Fourteenth Street.

Senneterre has grown well beyond its rail roots, with Resolute Forest Products providing employment at its mill and faster highway access to the lower Laurentians and Montreal. The improved highway system has extended the town's drawing area well to the west, spelling economic doom to the many smaller railway villages that grew around the stations of the NTR, although places like Amos and Macamic have retained their stations and continue to thrive. Other divisional points like Taschereau, however, have lost everything except a solitary track.

Garneau Junction

In 1906 the unstoppable Canadian Northern Railway began its invasion of Quebec, acquiring lines like the Quebec and Lac-Saint-Jean line and the Carillon and Grenville Railway. Within a few years, the CNoR (or Canadian Northern Quebec Railway, its regional name) had assembled a network of lines that linked Quebec City with Ottawa, and Montreal with the Lac-Saint-Jean region and the St. Lawrence River. The many routes came together at a place called Garneau Junction, situated a short distance from Grand-Mère. From Garneau Junction tracks led east to Quebec City, northeast to Lac-Saint-Jean, south to Cap-de-la-Madeleine near Trois-Rivières, and west to Montreal and Ottawa.

Like most divisional points, the site included a roundhouse, engine house, coal chute, and station. The modest community was laid out on a network of streets to the north of yards, not far from the nearby village of St. George. By 1980 the only remaining line was that from Montreal to Lac-Saint-Jean and Senneterre.

In some ways Garneau Junction has been forgotten by time. Along Ninety-Ninth Street, east of Highway 153, are a number of small railway homes, as well as a pair of former hotels, including the historic Bar Central. Unfortunately, the old "main street" on which the hotels sit has been boarded off from the tracks, so it is no longer possible to see any train activity from that point. The grid street pattern continues west of the 153 (which in fact bisected the village to construct a bridge over the tracks), although most of the homes along these roads are of much more recent vintage.

Still, the yards contain a two-track engine house, with the VIA station situated in the dispatch office; however, it is unlikely that it is a well-frequented stop. Although most of the remaining historic yard features no longer stand, the marshalling yard is one of the CNR's busiest in the region.

Farnham

Farnham is today a busy and attractive town situated in Quebec's Eastern Townships. Although its rail heritage is only a minor aspect of the town's makeup, those roots remain evident.

Farnham's railway days date back to 1853, when the Stanstead Shefford and Chambly Railway was chartered to serve a three-county area. Five years later a bridge over the Richelieu River at Saint-Jean allowed the SS&C to link with the Champlain and St. Lawrence Railway. The following year the SS&C built a Y-shaped junction and engine house in Farnham.

But it was the South Eastern Railway that gave the fledgling railway town its biggest boost. Incorporated in 1871, the SER established its headquarters in Farnham, adding a new three-storey brick station with a two-storey tower on top, offices, engine house, and car and locomotive shops, and went on to acquire seven railway charters. By 1882 seven rail lines radiated out from Farnham with eighteen passenger trains calling daily. The following year the network was acquired by the CPR and became an important location on the CPR's Short Line from Montreal to Saint John, New Brunswick.

In 1949 the grand brick station burned and was replaced with a plainer two-storey International style station (see chapter 3) that remains today, designated under the HRSPA.

By the 1970s, however, Farnham's railway fortunes were declining. The repair shops, the roundhouse, the turntable, and the express and baggage offices were all removed, and in 1980 the last passenger train pulled away from the station. Finally, only one line remained, that of the Montreal to Saint John route. In 2002 the line was acquired by the Montreal Maine and Atlantic, which operated the route until a deadly derailment in Lac-Mégantic in 2013 destroyed that town's core and killed forty-seven people. The current owner is the Central Maine and Quebec Railway.

Today, while the town has outgrown its rail roots, the brick station still dominates the rail yard. Those yards continue to hum and throb with the diesels of the new rail company. Railway housing remains on the grid streets south of the station, while to the north side, the historic old main street ends at the tracks. A tourist office reflects a station architectural style while near it a display diesel sits beside a short rail trail, part of the line which led to Granby and beyond.

Mount Royal: The CNoR's Model City

It had no roundhouse, no coal dock, nor even a particularly large station. Yet Mount Royal's heritage roots are pure railway. In 1913 the Canadian Northern Railway, the dream of railway builders William Mackenzie and Donald Mann, was in its heyday. They had nearly completed a cross country railway that could compete with the legendary CPR. But a mountain stood in the way, and that mountain was Mount Royal in the middle of Montreal. Solution: tunnel under it (see chapter 6). Their tunnel station was to be on the southeastern face of the mountain on the northwestern fringes of downtown Montreal. But it was at the tunnel's northern exit that a large open tract of land invited them to create a model town.

In the centre of the plan was to stand the Mount Royal CNoR station. Surrounded by parkland, the station would be the focus of a converging network of streets. To create their dream town, Mackenzie and Mann hired noted landscape architect Frederick Gage Todd. The whole scheme unfolded in three phases, the first in 1914. The main thoroughfare, however, would remain the rail line itself, located below grade in a wide ditch.

The new town strictly regulated what could be built where and how big. Residential streets were to be twenty metres wide and business streets twenty-four metres. A twenty-metre boulevard encircles the site along its thirteen large parks. Lot sizes and housing styles were also spelled out in detail. In the plan, two main boulevards crossed diagonally at a large central park beside the station. From the park, streets radiate in several directions. The park, now Place du Centenaire, sits across from original station and welcomes arriving passengers with a landscaped flower garden.

Not too surprisingly, much has changed, as many of the earlier structures near the core area have been replaced by newer and larger apartments and businesses. Still, wide avenues like Laird Boulevard and Graham Boulevard, which radiate from the station, retain a landscaped boulevard down their centre, and

within a few blocks of the centre lead to the leafy early residential districts. The original station now houses a Pizzaiola restaurant, as well as access to the commuter train platform below and to city bus platforms.

A number of the streets reflect not only the names of early CNoR executives such as Laird, Kindersley, Lazard, and Kenaston, but the station platform located at the exit from the tunnel, now goes by Canora (CAnadian NOrthern RAilway)

RAILWAY TOWNS OF THE MARITIMES

Cape Tormentine

Cape Tormentine, just over twenty kilometres by boat to PEI, was the point from which goods and people would embark for the Island. In 1888 the tracks of the New Brunswick and PEI Railway arrived at the cape from its link with the ICR in Sackville, but shipment to the Island still depended upon the weather and the ice. Finally, railcar ferry service began in 1917 from Cape Tormentine to Borden on PEI and the terminus of the railway line there. The rails were extended to a new wharf while the CNR added a new station, and the town site began to develop on a small network of streets.

The rail yards included sidings, a water tower, and a two-stall roundhouse with a turntable. Cars and trains were ferried across the Northumberland Strait on the SS *Prince Edward Island*. After the PEI Railway was abandoned in 1988, the trains stopped running into Cape Tormentine. However, vehicular traffic continued to pour into the village until 1997 when the new Confederation Bridge was opened to

Once the rail ferry terminal between New Brunswick and Prince Edward Island, the village of Cape Tormentine, New Brunswick, retains a surprisingly complete collection of railway structures, including a roundhouse, water tower, and station.

the Island. For a period, the station functioned as a tourist information centre, but with no tourists, that function faded, and the station sits vacant.

Surprisingly, the station (a standard CN style — wooden with low hip roof and small gable trackside), roundhouse, and water tower remain in place, but for how much longer depends upon the heritage pride of the local community. The turntable itself has gone, although

the pit remains visible, and no tracks remain. The right of way has become the Tantramar Rail Trail from Sackville, and the homes are now primarily those of local fishermen and summer residents. Repurposing the site as a rail attraction with a track and a railway equipment display would help bring some tourist traffic back into this fading community, not just as a side trip from the bridge, but also from cyclists using the historic and scenic rail trail.

Napadogan

Once a busy NTR divisional point between Moncton and Edmunston, Napadogan is now a virtual ghost town. In 1912 the NTR chose a remote location for its divisional facilities in what was then a forested region in central New Brunswick. The townsite displayed the standard grid network of streets, identical to those the railway created across the Prairies and in much of northern Quebec and Ontario. The yards contained coaling dock, water tower, and a crew house. Small houses were built along the half dozen streets. The station was built in the standard NTR plan — two storeys with a hip-gable roof and small central gable above the operator's bay. The second floor contained quarters for the agent and other railway employees.

The station burned in 1968 and was replaced with a small modern aluminum shed. By then however, the divisional town functions were no longer needed, as steam had been replaced by diesel power, and by 1998 all railway structures had been removed ... except the roundhouse, constructed of brick and now part of a veneer plant. Meanwhile, the streets are lined with overgrown lots with only a handful of homes remaining, some vacant. Although passenger trains have long since stopped calling, the line remains in use with CN freight traffic.

Aroostook Junction

Like Napadogan, the CPR divisional point of Aroostook Junction is, for the most part, a railway ghost town. Although a string of homes still line Highway 130 and a few back streets, the site of the railway structures is vacant with no evidence that they ever existed. Only the station has managed to survive. Although decrepit and heavily overgrown, there are local plans to revive it as part of the Trans-Canada Trail, which follows the roadbed. Beyond the station grounds, the trail crosses an unusual curving bridge over the Aroostook River. The trail and the site of the railway structures lie on a river flat below the current village homes.

The station is deceptively small for being a divisional station. It is but a single storey, wood, with a small gable above the bay and hip gable ends to the roof. The station was built in 1906 and is designated station under the HRSPA.

One of Canada's earliest rail lines, the New Brunswick and Canada Railway opened its line between St. Andrews and Debec in 1857. Twenty years later the line was extended across the St. John River and on into Edmunston. From Aroostook the line was extended across the border into Maine. In 1895 that branch was extended to join the CPR deeper into Maine, becoming the Bangor and Aroostook Railway.

When the CPR acquired the lines in the area it established Aroostook Junction as a divisional point. At its busiest, Aroostook Junction could claim, besides the station, six duplex tenements for staff, a bunkhouse, bungalows for the station master and his assistants, a section house, freight sheds, a roundhouse, and turntable located across the tracks from the station. In 1982 the CPR abandoned its route between McAdam and Edmunston. When it did, a number of other stations remained standing, including those at Woodstock, Florenceville, Bath, Perth Andover, Grand Falls, and Edmunston. Today, the stations at Edmunston (a museum), Bath (a residence), Grand Falls (vacant), Aroostook, and Florenceville (relocated but preserved) still survive (see chapter 3).

The now nearly abandoned divisional town of Aroostook, New Brunswick, still retains its modest station (shown here in the 1980s), now a designated structure and currently heavily overgrown.

McAdam

The unassuming little community of McAdam may well be Canada's ultimate railway town. Not only does it contain what is possibly Canada's most magnificent railway station (see chapter 3), but most of the structures were built by CPR, and, most importantly, all are treasured and celebrated by this proud little town.

At first there was the New Brunswick and Canada Railway, built inland from the port of St. Andrews.

When the CPR built its Short Line from Montreal through Maine to Saint John, New Brunswick, it established a junction at the remote community of McAdam. Meanwhile, down at St. Andrews, the Algonquin Inn was beginning to attract tourists who would take the CPR from Montreal or from Boston and transfer at McAdam. In response, the CPR built a Chateau-style, three-storey station/hotel to accommodate the wealthy clientele.

More than just the Chateauesque station, McAdam, New Brunswick, has retained much of its railway heritage, including the grand home of the master mechanic, and several other designated railway homes.

The company then built more than thirty-three houses for its staff. Many of them were designed by the CPR's own architect, Edward Maxwell. With the rugged terrain, the streets were unable to follow the standard grid pattern and the resulting roads follow a somewhat circuitous route. Along them most of the CPR housing still solidly stands. In fact, a number are registered heritage properties.

The storey-and-a-half Klondike house, with its mansard roof, is one of a string of ten such homes. Another designated home is the master mechanic's house, situated across the road from the station. Naturally, it is a much grander home than those for the other employees, as the master mechanic was usually the most important person among the employees. This well preserved two-storey house contains servants' quarters, two living rooms, two fireplaces with shell cased ceramic tiles, wrought iron chandeliers, as well as a large yard and exterior ornamentation.

A more typical residence is the two-storey duplex situated on Lake Street, one of a row of double tenement homes, again designed by Edward Maxwell in 1899. It, too, is a designated heritage structure. Throughout the community sits the railway housing, including a very early crew quarters which dates from before the arrival of the CPR. Indeed, the original simple wooden McAdam station still survives on a side street and it too is designated.

A local commission has been tasked with the preservation of this McAdam's railway heritage. The Irving family, of oil fame in the province, has donated much of their railway property to the town and periodically operates a charitable train excursion with vintage coaches that they keep in Saint John. McAdam is a short drive from Fredericton and from the U.S. border and is worthy of the attention it has earned and the visitors it attracts.

Although once a major railway hub for the DAR, Kentville, Nova Scotia, has lost its railway heritage, leaving this mural to give that heritage a nominal nod.

Kentville

This busy town was once the headquarters for the Dominion Atlantic Railway, with a large station and office building, yards, a roundhouse, and the usual array of divisional railway structures. None of this survives. When the CPR folded its tent and abandoned the line in 1990, the town demolished the grand station/office, built in 1869 and a designated heritage structure. Because VIA was briefly running its trains from Halifax to Yarmouth, it added a single-storey brick station with small tower. That service was discontinued in 1990. The building now houses a tourist bureau.

Although the roundhouse outlasted the transition from steam to diesel, and was touted for preservation, the town council buckled to pressure from a developer, and in 2007 ordered its demolition. Organized protests from the Roundhouse Action Group and a 130-name petition failed to prevent this short-sighted decision. The five-stall brick roundhouse was built in 1916 and employed one-third of the town's railway employees.

Even the survival of the grand Cornwallis railway hotel (see chapter 5) is questionable.

THE SATELLITE TOWNS

Throughout much of eastern Canada, the railways kept their stations away from existing towns and villages due either to high land costs or simply because they were in the wrong place to accommodate a station (i.e. hills and water availability). One needs only to look at a road map to see locations which include the word "station" or "junction" in their place name to determine where these are. Few retain their original stations, nor the buildings which served them such as hotels and crew housing.

Among the few that evoke the days of rail are Oxford Junction, Nova Scotia, on the former ICR main line, and the former branch to Oxford and Tatamagouche. Near the junction of the tracks a few early workers' homes yet linger, although the station and other railway structures are gone. Pugwash Junction formed the link with the branch to Pugwash, and here, too, a few early buildings remain.

In New Brunswick, Fredericton Junction displays a few railway-era homes along the grid streets, and also contains a modern-style station operated by the New Brunswick Southern Railway. Until its historic (and designated) station disappeared, Canterbury ranked among the most authentic of the satellite villages, one that outgrew its parent village. A few of the older buildings, likely hotels or boarding houses, still stand by the now-abandoned roadbed.

Several station villages appeared throughout the province of Quebec, but modernization has removed or covered over most of the early rail-related homes and shops. The junction towns of Tring-Jonction and Vallée-Jonction have managed to retain their historic stone stations, although the towns have outgrown their rail roots. Near the Vallée-Jonction station, many structures have survived, including a roundhouse with turntable intact, a through-truss railway bridge, a railway hotel (now a restaurant), and an iron footbridge leading across the tracks from the main part of the town that sits high above on a ridge. To round out the image, a railway display including steam engine sits on nearby tracks (see chapter 7).

Although lacking tracks and rail trails, Stanbridge Station offers a streetscape of early rail-era buildings, as do Sainte-Rose station and Sainte-Sabine station. The old CPR station was moved from Stanbridge to the grounds of the Champlain Industries where it became a storage shed.

In Newfoundland, with its many branch lines, several communities grew into junctions with a mere handful of homes for workers. Due to their remote locations, few remain inhabited.

One junction village that has survived in Newfoundland is Whitbourne. From it, many of the branch lines were opened even before the main line was completed. The line to Harbour Grace from Whitbourne was opened in 1883, later extended to Carbonear and Baie Verte. One of its early names was Harbour Grace Junction.

Three hotels catered to travellers who were transferring to the branch lines and for railway crews as well. At this time, Robert Reid, owner of the Reid Newfoundland Railway, established the line's headquarters here and changed the name to Whitbourne to honour colonist Sir Richard Whitbourne. In 1890 Reid added a roundhouse, engine and car shops, and a large two-storey wooden station. When the headquarters moved to St. John's, Whitbourne began a slow decline in population. The old station burned and was replaced with a newer CN-style building with a single storey and hip gable roof ends. Meanwhile, all other railway buildings were removed. Only the station remains.

Today, now repurposed, the station houses the municipal office and a small museum while a train display sits outside. In 1998 the CN Pensioners Association raised funds to erect a monument to the memory of railroaders who were killed on duty. Many of the homes on the village streets are of more recent vintage. A pair of rough gravel trails mark the locations of the branches that emanated from the station town.

THE CASTLES OF THE LINE: THE RAILWAY HOTELS

5

Even from the earliest days of rail travel, passengers needed accommodation whether awaiting a connecting train or staying in town for business. Most of the earliest railway hotels were simple wooden structures, resembling their predecessor stage coach hotels. But as rail companies competed to attract more passengers, the hotels improved. And then it occurred to the ambitious president of the CPR, William Cornelius Van Horne, that his new coast-to-coast railway passed through some impressive scenery. Then, with the fortuitous discovery of hot springs by his workers, Van Horne quickly recognized the tourist potential his line offered and began construction of the Chateau-style Banff Springs Hotel. And with that, Canada's railways entered the tourist business.

While most railway hotels were built close to urban stations, such as Toronto's Royal York, Victoria's Empress Hotel, and Halifax's Nova Scotian, others took full advantage of their bucolic rural settings to attract vacationers. Thus we have Nova Scotia's Digby Pines, Cape Breton's Grand Narrows Hotel, the Chateau Montebello in Quebec (although it was not initially a railway hotel), Quebec City's lofty Chateau Frontenac, and the Algonquin Inn in St. Andrews, New Brunswick. Happily, unlike many of the stations they served, the railway hotel heritage of Quebec and the Atlantic provinces remains to help modern vacationers enjoy the ambience of early rail travel.

THE RAILWAY HOTELS OF QUEBEC

A Castle on a Cliff: The Mighty Chateau Frontenac

William Cornelius Van Horne, the CPR's feisty president, had a sound bite for every building the CPR built. For the grand Banff Springs Hotel in the stunning Rocky Mountains, he stated that if he couldn't bring the scenery to the tourists, he would take the tourists to the scenery; he declared the CPR's Windsor Station in Montreal "the best station in all creation." As for the Chateau Frontenac, he claimed it would be the "most talked about hotel on the continent."

The Chateau Frontenac hotel in Quebec City, now in the Fairmont chain, was the CPR's finest hotel in eastern Canada, and continues to attract many visitors to this walled city.

The site, strategically perched on a high cliff overlooking the St. Lawrence River, was a natural spot for Samuel de Champlain to construct Fort St. Louis in 1620. In 1636 the first governor of New France, Charles de Montmagny, replaced the fort with his home, the Chateau St. Louis. Then, after its destruction by William Phipps in 1690, it was rebuilt by the Comte de Frontenac in 1692. After that burned down in 1834, Lord Durham covered the ruins with the Dufferin Terrace, where visitors stroll today to view the vast river and mountain scenery. In recent years, the foundations of the 1636 chateau have been exposed beneath the Terrace and are available for tourists to view.

In 1892, anxious to follow on the success of the western chateaus, Van Horne, along with Donald Smith and Thomas Shaugnessy, formed the Chateau Frontenac

Company, and put the CPR's prolific architect Bruce Price to work to design a French Renaissance chateau perched prominently on the cliff. Opened in December of 1893, the chateau exceeded all expectations. Using blue limestone and Glenboig brick, the structure took the form of a horseshoe, its four wings linked by towers. Of the 170 rooms, ninety-three boasted private bathrooms with marble fixtures.

As demand boomed, new wings were added, as well as a seventeen-storey central tower, bringing the number of rooms to 658. In 1973, and again in 1989, the CPR undertook extensive renovations to the facilities and the guest rooms, but left its iconic profile unaltered. Inside, much history continues to survive, such as the Palm Room, what is now the Champlain Restaurant, and the Riverview wing. Expansion of the kitchen, however, led to the burial of the original stone arch entrance. The hotel is now a part of the Fairmount hotel network.

Many a historic figure has travelled to the chateau from the CPR's stunning Gare du Palais station, including Kings George V and VI, Queen Elizabeth II, while Charles Lindberg flew in to visit a sick friend. American presidents Roosevelt, Eisenhower, and Nixon have all been guests. Numerous heads of state trouped through during the spectacular Expo '67 held in Montreal.

And to celebrate the man who dreamed the dream, a suite has been named in honour of Van Horne himself.

A Log Castle: The Chateau Montebello

What the Chateau Montebello lacks in Chateau architecture, it more than compensates in its stunning log construction.

The property originated, as did many in Quebec, as a seigneury, this one granted in 1674 by the French king to Bishop Laval of Quebec City. In 1854, with the property then in the hands of the Papineau family, the seigneurial system was abolished. Louis Joseph Papineau chose to call the land Monte-bello, named after his manor house (which still stands as a historic property nearby).

The chateau itself originates with American entrepreneur H.M. Saddlemire, who wanted a wilderness retreat for himself and his wealthy friends. The large site on the Ottawa River was exactly what he was looking for. Bankrolled in part by William Beatty, president of the CPR, Saddlemire began construction in March of 1930. Using his Scandinavian background, he employed a log-building technique previously unknown in Canada. Scandinavian experts worked along with Quebec loggers, sleeping on site in boxcars, to complete the massive hotel in a mere four months as western red cedars, many as long as twenty metres, arrived by the trainload, ten thousand in all.

When it opened in July, visitors were amazed at the soaring six-sided stone fireplace, which extended four storeys in the middle of the foyer. Four wings lead off from the foyer. Nearby, a dining room extended four storeys. An indoor pool, the largest of its kind at the time, opened in 1931, and included a hand-painted ceiling, still surviving today. Many large historic-themed murals by renowned muralist Adam Sherriff Scott (1887–1980) appear throughout the building.

The vast property, known at first as the Seigneury Club, contained several small lakes where guests could relax in private chalets. These guests included celebrities and royalty alike, among them Bing Crosby, Bette Davis and Perry Como, Prince Ranier and Princess Grace of Monaco, and Crown Princess Juliana of the Netherlands.

In 1970 the Seigneury Club became a CPR hotel, with a new name, the Chateau Montebello. The train station itself reflected the log style of the hotel, with a high ceiling in the waiting room and naturally a large stone fireplace. It now rests in a new location on the village main street, serving as a tourist centre and choclaterie.

One of the fascinating architectural features of the Fairmont Chateau Montebello hotel in Gatineau, Quebec, is the lofty six-sided stone fireplace that rises up through the centre of the lobby.

La Seigneurie Triton

No sooner had the rails of the Quebec and Lake St. John (now Lac-Saint-Jean) Railway opened, than a train engineer named Alexander Luders Light realized a dream. Here, in the then remote forests of northern Quebec, fish and game abounded. Now that these areas had rail access, Light reasoned, fishermen and hunters would ride the rails to visit the region. And so in 1886, near a rail trestle across Batiscan River, Light founded the Triton Fish and Game Club.

Just seven years later a wooden clubhouse welcomed its first visitors. While the Triton is not a railway hotel in the sense that the CPR's magnificent chateaus are, nor a railway-operated camp like the CPR's bungalow camp on Ontario's French River, it remained accessible only by rail, and the brainchild of a true railway man. And his destination attracted the kings of industry and the heads of state. Churchill, Truman, and Roosevelt were among the early guests, as were the Rockefellers and the Molsons.

In many ways little has changed. The attractive wooden clubhouse still stands as it has since 1893, with its wooden staircases and wainscoting. No telephones ring, no TVs blare numbing commercials, no one stares at computer screens as there is no Wi-Fi.

Visitors still arrive by rail on VIA Rail's Saguenay train, disembarking at a small wooden shed that serves as a station. Here by a large window they meet the club representative and follow a path down to the river where a two kilometre boat ride glides them to their remote quarters on Lac La Croix. In the century-old clubhouse they encounter early photos, artifacts such as an early telephone, and the hall of presidents. The lodge spreads across three wings, the central hall rising two-and-a-half storeys. Steep gables encompass half-timber exteriors. Guests may then be led

A parking lot has replaced the train sheds which stood at the rear entrance to the grand Gare Viger hotel and station built by the CPR in Montreal.

to their room in the lodge where they share showers and washrooms, or to a more recent pavilion or chalet with private facilities. Tipis offer an opportunity to spend time living as the early First Nations inhabitants might.

The Triton is no longer the exclusive domain of the hunter and fisher; families may now enjoy hiking twenty kilometres of trail, or canoeing or fishing within the 420-square-kilometre forest preserve, where the distant rumble of a VIA train reminds them of the resort's roots.

La Place Viger Hotel

Montreal's successes at preserving its railway heritage have been mixed. While the demolition of historic treasures like the Van Horne mansion and the old Bonaventure station are blemishes on Montreal's heritage preservation efforts, the Westmount station and the Place Viger station-hotel, despite degradation, remain defiantly in place.

At La Place Viger, CPR trains arriving from Quebec City or northern Quebec would come to rest by the train sheds at the rear of the hotel where travellers would then be escorted into the palatial splendour of another of CPR architect Bruce Price's Chateau creations. A large tower dominated the centre portion while smaller towers and dormers marked various corners and the roof. The steeply pitched roof was covered with copper, the building itself made of stone.

La Place Viger opened in 1898. Six storeys high, the hotel offered eighty-eight rooms. Once inside, travellers would encounter a fine dining restaurant. Capacity was expanded with an addition in 1913. In front of the hotel stood the magnificent Viger Gardens, with ornamental gardens, shady trees, walkways, and a bandstand where military bands played in the afternoon sun. Inside was music of a different kind, as popular orchestras played the latest in jazz and dance tunes.

In 1939 the hotel closed (although the station functioned for another dozen years) when the city took it over, converting the once-elegant interior into a warren of offices for bureaucrats. Behind the building, the tracks and train sheds became a parking lot.

Sadly, the gardens, too, fell victim to insensitive change, and were dug up for a buried expressway. In 1995 the government of Quebec extended the boundaries of the Vieux-Montreal historic district to include La Place Viger. By 2014, the government had moved out and the building was up for lease.

The Queen Elizabeth Hotel and the Chateau Champlain

Hotels of such modern design and with little to do directly with the railways are only marginally considered part of the railroad heritage. But both the Queen Elizabeth Hotel and the Chateau Champlain were built by railway companies and linked to two of Montreal's most important stations.

Completed in 1958 by the Canadian National Railways, the twenty-one storey Queen Elizabeth Hotel, with its 1,200 rooms, became a frequent source of controversy. First, of course, was the name. Among francophone Quebeckers it was not a popular choice. The Ligue d'action national urged that the name Chateau Maisonneuve be used, but neither a two-thousand-name petition nor five hundred demonstrators burning the CNR president in effigy effected a change. The Quebec crisis of 1970, when the Front de Liberation de Quebec (FLQ) kidnapped two politicians (killing one), turned the hotel into army headquarters while soldiers sought the kidnappers.

Only two peaceful years earlier, however, John Lennon and Yoko Ono moved into a seventeenth floor room where with many of their friends they recorded the iconic protest song, "Give Peace a Chance."

Unfortunately, despite its modernistic elegance, the hotel rose atop the Gare Centrale, entombing the station's exterior features and turning the new station into little more than a subterranean concourse.

The CPR's Chateau Champlain, however, pleased Quebeckers with not only its name, but also with the fact that it was the first hotel to be designed by a francophone Quebec architectural firm, namely the firm of D'Aston and Poirtier. The thirty-eight-storey hotel was originally intended to form part of a grander Place du Canada, which would have meant the demolition of the CPR's own historic Windsor Station. In this case protests were more successful, and the station was saved while the scale of the hotel was reduced. Its distinctive style displays a domed roof and windows with curved tops, giving it a space age futuristic appearance. It stands across the road from the Windsor Station, which no longer sees train service.

LeGrand Hotel

Overlooking the Atlantic Ocean on the Gaspé Peninsula, LeGrand hotel in Port-Daniel was built in 1898 by Alfred LeGrand. The hotel predates the construction of the Atlantic Quebec and Western Railway, but when the track layers reached Port-Daniel, they had to wait while a tunnel was blasted through the stubborn rocks further along. During that period the hotel essentially became a railway hotel, and remained so once the trains started calling at the nearby station.

The two-storey wooden structure, with its mansard roof and dormers of bright silver tin, offered twenty-six rooms and was among the region's most popular tourist accommodations. Sadly, in the mid-1900s the hotel stood vacant and in serious disrepair. Then a local group known as Les Amis de L'hotel Grand (Friends of the LeGrand Hotel) raised enough capital to restore the building. La Maison LeGrand now houses the local library, and a small museum dedicated to the LeGrand family and the building, as does an interpretive plaque on the grounds.

THE RAILWAY HOTELS OF NOVA SCOTIA

The Nova Scotian

It was the most prominent feature that immigrants arriving to Canada's shore might have seen from the deck of their ship as it inched to the dock at Pier 21. Here, the newcomers would be processed before boarding their trains to their strange new destinations. But the eight-storey Nova Scotian hotel may also have delivered a short respite after the long ocean voyage.

Following the deadly Halifax explosion of 1917, which killed nearly two thousand Haligonians and injured thousands more, rebuilding the city quickly became a priority. During the 1920s the newly created Canadian National Railway set out to compete with its rival the CPR in establishing a string of grand railway hotels. The Nova Scotian was to be one of their finest.

Completed in 1930, the hotel commanded views of both the harbour to the north and the immaculate Cornwallis Garden to the south especially from its eighth-floor tearoom. The Evangeline Restaurant boasted tuxedoed waiters and fine china and silverware, while the Eager Beaver bar provided more relaxed atmosphere. Built of brick and sandstone, the eight-storey hotel offered 180 guestrooms finished in mahogany; the bathrooms had cigar rests.

Not only would the hotel have easy access for sea-borne arrivals, but the new CNR station was joined to the east end of the hotel by a short passageway. Royal visitors included King George VI and the Queen mother in 1939, Queen Elizabeth in the 1950s and again in the 1970s, and Diana, Princess of Wales, in the 1980s, as well as baseball legend Babe Ruth.

The hotel was enlarged in the late 1950s. Closed in 1993, its future appeared uncertain. Three years later New Castle Hotels and Resorts saved the hotel by pumping fifteen million dollars into renovations and restorations.

Halifax's Westin Nova Scotian Hotel is affixed to the neoclassical VIA train station.

Now a Westin hotel, the Nova Scotian can yet display many heritage features from its early glory days. The lobby retains its original ambience with marble columns and copper leaf ceiling features. The original back entrance, however, is now occupied by a swimming pool. Brass railings still extend from the lower level to the main floor. The grand ballroom features original fixtures and plaster work, even the kitchen retains the early chef's station.

Outside, the nearby Pier 21 museum has become a moving tribute to the plight of Canada's immigrant arrivals. The station has retained its classical splendor, although government cutbacks have reduced VIA arrivals to only three a week.

The Lord Nelson

It may seem odd that the CPR would construct a hotel where it had no station. However, that rail company also owned the Dominion Atlantic Railway, which wished to have a hotel property where its customers could access an ocean port. The DAR operated a daily passenger train from Halifax's CN station to Yarmouth where passengers could board a steamship bound for Boston. Although a CPR railway company, the DAR enjoyed running rights over the CNR from Halifax to Windsor Junction.

Opened in 1928, the Lord Nelson was seven storeys high, offered two hundred guest rooms, and was considered the province's grandest hotel at the time. Construction material was primarily local and used bluenose brick over a concrete frame. A treed, semi-circular driveway offered access from South Park Street. A pair of towers was added in the 1960s and 1970s.

Among the hotel's surviving heritage features are a gold leaf ceiling in the lobby, a copy of that in Ottawa's house of commons, along with floral motifs and a CPR logo. The ballroom retains its original hardwood floors and crystal chandeliers.

Celebrity guests have included Anne Murray, the Rolling Stones, and Sir Paul McCartney. A prominent wartime guest was Admiral Emile Muselier, who, as part of General Charles de Gaulle's exiled French government, used the hotel to plot the re-taking of the French islands of St. Pierre and Miquelon, located just off the coast of Newfoundland and then part of occupied France. While his success did not turn the tide of the war, it did offer a much needed morale boost to the beleaguered French.

The Grand Narrows Hotel

The Grand Narrows Hotel, situated on the scenic shores of the Bras d'Or Lakes, was built in conjunction with the construction of the government-owned Intercolonial Railway across Cape Breton Island. Its state of preservation and

No longer a railway accommodation, the Grand Narrows Hotel is now a popular bed and breakfast on the shores of the scenic Bras D'or Lakes in central Cape Breton Island.

its scenic location make it one of eastern Canada's most attractive hotel locations. It is said that when Prime Minister John A. Macdonald was staying at the hotel, he looked across the narrows and declared that this was the location where his government would locate the railway bridge. And in 1890, when the first train chugged across the seven-span steel structure, none other than Governor General Lord Stanley was at the throttle.

Edward McNeil and Hector McDougall were the hotel's promoters and builders. The building style is considered Second Empire, with its mansard roof, two-storey verandah, and central door with transom and sidelights. The white clapboard hotel rises three and a half storeys and rests on a rubble stone foundation. As well, the building retains much of its interior wood trim around windows doors and staircases.

The building looks over the Grand Narrows of the Bras d'Or Lakes and is surrounded by rolling pastoral countryside. The train station, now long gone, was designed on the same pattern as that surviving at Orangedale. Although freight trains still rumble across the bridge, Grand Narrows has not seen passenger service since VIA Rail was forced to discontinue the tourist train, the *Bras d'Or*, a decade ago. The hotel, a designated heritage property, remains in use as a popular bed and breakfast.

The Cornwallis Inn

No one who visits the busy town of Kentville, Nova Scotia, would mistake it for having once been one of the province's most important railway towns, as most of that heritage has been removed. Western Nova Scotia's main rail operator was the Dominion Atlantic Railway, which operated from Halifax to Yarmouth. Its main hub was Kentville, with offices in the grand two-storey station which was the focus of the maintenance shops, yards, and roundhouse. The station was replaced a few decades ago with smaller, more modern building, complete with a small decorative tower. It is now a tourist information centre. The roundhouse was demolished within the last decade, despite strong local objections, to make way for a chain retail store. No tracks remain. It is as if the place had no railway heritage at all.

But then there is the Cornwallis Inn.

In 1919 the DAR purchased the Aberdeen Hotel, remodelling it and renaming it the Cornwallis Inn. In 1930 the railway replaced the old hotel completely with a new ninety-room structure. The five-storey, Tudoresque brick building featured a row of arched windows along the rotunda and a castellated corner tower. Ivy covered the walls and a landscaped garden graced the front.

But then in 1973, major renovations altered the grand building, converting the guest rooms into apartments while much of the main floor became offices and a bar. The garden became a parking lot.

Still, a surprising amount of original heritage features survive. Among them are the brass mail box, brass elevator doors, wood trim, and wainscoting, the fireplace in the lobby along with a crest on the walls, and door and window features. Despite their survival, these features appear only minimally maintained. Still, in a town that seems to have rejected its railway roots, the Cornwallis Inn is a heritage treasure.

Much of the interior of the Cornwallis Inn displays traditional features.

The elegant former CPR Cornwallis Inn in Kentville, Nova Scotia, still shows off its glory, and is now apartments, offices, and a bar.

Digby Pines

Less well-known than many of its other chateau hotels, the CPR's Digby Pines, in Digby, Nova Scotia, was nonetheless as grand and as popular as its more renowned chateau palaces. Built in 1905 by Henry Churchill, the hotel was then bought by the Dominion Atlantic Railway (part of the CPR empire) which brought travellers to the scenic bayside locale. In 1928 the CPR demolished the original wooden building, replacing it with a three-storey structure in a modified Chateau style with steeply pitched roofs and a tower.

Lured by the scenic views of the Digby Gap, the fishing, and especially the pollen-free air, visitors arrived by train from New York and Boston on the *New Yorker* or the *Bluenose*, or on the CPR's own trains from across eastern Canada. Weekly ships also arrived from New York. In 1965 the government of Nova Scotia acquired the property, which includes thirty-one cottages, and continues to operate it as a hotel. Neither ships nor trains call any more as travellers today arrive by the decidedly less glamorous automobile.

OTHER GRAND RAILWAY HOTELS OF THE MARITIMES

The Algonquin Resort

The Algonquin Resort, in St. Andrews, New Brunswick, began not as a railway hotel, but rather a seaside escape from the dust and pollen which made Montreal summers a choking hell. With its "no mosquito" boast and clean drinking water, the hotel was an instant success.

Guests at first arrived by train on the New Brunswick Railway. Following that line's takeover by the CPR, the new owners built a grand station-hotel at McAdam, New Brunswick, to allow for a luxurious transfer to the St. Andrews train.

In 1902 the CPR purchased the eighty-room hotel and added a golf course. When the old wooden structure burned to the ground in 1914, the CPR created a much grander building using a version of its popular Chateau style, with two prominent towers and steep rooflines. It even received a new brand, becoming "St. Andrews by-the-Sea." Although the trains stopped bringing the tourists in 1958, improved highways kept the crowds coming.

The hotel's ownership has gone back and forth. In the 1970s the CPR sold the hotel to local interests which in turn sold it to the New Brunswick government. The government, in turn, allowed the CPR to continue managing and marketing the property. Between 1991 and 2001 a new wing, spa, and rooftop garden were added. In 2014, following two years of major renovation, it reopened as the Marriot chain's first Autograph Collection property in Canada. With new features such as a waterslide, the once summer-only resort has become a year-round attraction.

A tree-lined boulevard leads from the entrance of the building to the shore where visitors would disembark from the trains. The former CPR station, a surprisingly simple wooden building, still stands near its original site.

The town itself is a heritage treasure trove with a main street of historic wooden buildings, many more than century old, all lining Passamaquoddy Bay.

The Charlottetown Hotel

Following its creation and absorption of Canada's many bankrupt rail lines, the Canadian National Railways undertook a hotel-building initiative. When the Victoria Hotel burned in 1928, the city of Charlottetown, Prince Edward Island, was left with no elegant accommodations to attract tourists. The city approached CNR president Henry Thornton to build a new hotel.

John Schofield, the rail line's leading architect and designer of CNR's classical stations, created a red brick neo-Georgian beauty, eschewing the rival CPR's propensity toward French Chateau hotels.

In 1931 the five-storey, 110-room hotel opened on Kent Street. Visitors would enter into a lobby with a barrel-vaulted ceiling, marble floors, and wood trim. Crystal chandeliers hung from the ceiling of the

The trains no longer bring guests to the stunning and popular Algonquin Resort in St. Andrews, New Brunswick, yet its CPR roots are reflected in the grand Chateau style.

Georgian Room, a grand dining hall where the hotel band would provide the dance music. Today it serves as a banquet room with pillars and a decorative high ceiling. The Chambers Restaurant, too, has retained much of its elegant wall and ceiling features. The lobby bar displays rich wood trim both on the counter and around the mirror. Larger, more exclusive suites occupy the top floor.

The entranceway is through four double pillars topped with a coat of arms. Although the hotel is several blocks from the former train station (which still survives), it is close to the heritage buildings of Kent Street and Queen Street. The hotel is now a Rodd signature hotel.

SMALLER RAILWAY HOTELS

Across eastern Canada, local hotels frequently sprang up close to the countless small town train stations. Here, no grand Chateau style rose above the landscape. Rather, these locally built hostels were usually little more than two or three storeys, and were geared more toward travelling businessmen than vacationing tourists. While few have been accorded heritage status, the hotel in Salisbury, New Brunswick, is an exception.

Salisbury had one of the busiest stations on the European and North American Railway, an early line built between Saint John and Pointe-du-Chêne (Shediac). Within a few short years, a string of hotels appeared along the street by the station. In 1887 Patrick Gray built the Depot Railway Hotel on the site of the burnt-down McDonald Hotel. Built in a style known as Colonial Revival, the clapboard structure is two and half storeys with a central dormer. Although now a residence, it retains many of its architectural elements; however, a porch which formerly extended the width of the building is now missing. The building is now a designated heritage structure.

Rexton, New Brunswick, offers up another designated heritage hotel, the Kent Northern. The hotel was built following the arrival of the Kent Northern Railway in the 1880s. As originally built, the hotel consisted of two storeys, the second level being within its mansard roof. Following the CNR's takeover of the railway in 1929, the hotel became the Rexton Hotel. Today, it is no longer a hotel and its exterior has been modified most notably with the removal of the large verandah.

The busy mill town of Edmunston, New Brunswick, contains few heritage structures, but the former York Hotel is one. Built in 1913 by Georges Ringuette, it is simple in its architecture, being rectangular with only a flat roof. Situated directly across from the CNR's postwar station, it was intended to house rail crews and visitors alike. A fire in 1975 destroyed the upper floor of the four-storey structure, which in 1980 became an apartment building.

Despite having no heritage protection, many other railway communities can yet claim small railway-related hotel buildings. One of the more attractive such structures lies adjacent to the heritage station in Vallée-Jonction, Quebec. Now a popular bar and restaurant, it still retains many of its original exterior features including a prominent tower on the corner.

In the pretty seaside village of Caraquet, New Brunswick, stands the now upscale boutique hotel, the Hotel Paulin. Although not built by the railway, it stood close enough to the railway station to no doubt have served the train travellers. It dates from 1891, when it was known as the Hotel Vendome. It takes its present name from Octave and Annie Paulin, who acquired the building in 1907. Further restoration began in 1972, and the hotel is now classed as a four-star boutique hotel. With its front tower and seventeen dormers in the third floor mansard roof, it sits amid lovely landscaped grounds. The tracks and station have long gone, and the roadbed is now a cycling trail.

Opposite one of New Brunswick's most attractive stations is the hotel that served it. The aptly named Depot Hotel in Sussex, New Brunswick, was built in 1911 in a simple flat-roof style. The main portion is three storeys high, the extensions two storeys. The solid brick building, which now houses a restaurant, sits kitty-corner from the Sussex station.

Although neither remain as hotels, two buildings in the historic community of Hampton, New Brunswick, have served previously as railway hotels. The Wayside Apartments and the Red Brick Corner Restaurant, both three storeys high, lie across the tracks opposite the preserved 1930s train station, which is now a museum and gift shop.

Close by the Grand Trunk station in Saint-Hyacinthe, Quebec, sits the Bar Le Grand Tronc, while in Sherbrooke, Quebec, the Hotel Wellington rises behind the GTR station, which is now a bus terminal and restaurant.

In Victoriaville, Quebec, the Bar le Grand Union was built in 1889 directly across the tracks from the Grand Trunk station. An unusually attractive hotel, the three-storey building boasts a mansard roof and a four-storey tower above the entrance, also with a mansard roof. It sits on a short pedestrian-only street. A velogare has replaced the original station and provides shelter and facilities for cyclists on this popular rail trail.

A classical small-town railway landscape survives in Hampton, New Brunswick, with a station and a pair of former railway hotels.

The Hotel Mont Tremblant, directly across from the rebuilt CPR station in that the town of the same name, was erected in 1902, largely for workers at the local mill. But as alpine skiing surged in popularity in 1937, it became a haven for the hordes of skiers tumbling off *Le P'tit Train du Nord* from Montreal. Although trains no longer call, the region has remained a mecca for skiers in winter, while cyclists in summer stream along the rail trail that passes right by the station.

STRUCTURES: THE HIDDEN FACES OF THE RAILWAYS 6

Over the years, Canada's railways have relied on a great variety of railway structures and buildings. In addition to the thousands of stations, high bridges, and grand hotels, trains needed water towers at roughly thirty-kilometre intervals to slake the thirst of the steam engines, coal chutes at less frequent intervals to provide fuel, and roundhouses and engine and car shops for repair and maintenance of engines and coaches. Turntables, crossing towers, and warehouses, as well as offices for ticketing and for administration, are usually the forgotten faces of the railways. And, not surprisingly, few remain.

As railways evolved (or devolved, as the case may be) many of these support structures were no longer needed. Water towers and coal chutes are very scarce these days, and survive only because authorities haven't gotten around to ripping them down. If they weren't repurposed, warehouses didn't last much longer than most stations.

Roundhouses could be contentious. Because of their single function and locations in remote corners of the rail yards, preserving and repurposing them was difficult. The only successful preservations of roundhouses have been the John Street roundhouse in Toronto, which retains its turntable and displays historic rolling stock as part of the site's museum, and the CPR roundhouse in Vancouver built in 1888/1911, now an arts and community centre. A few other roundhouses have become part of industrial or commercial operations.

Office buildings may have been part of a station itself, such as at Senneterre, Farnham, or Kentville, or may have been a separate building, such as the QCR office in Sherbrooke.

Homes of the wealthy railway builders form a valuable part of railway heritage as well. Minister's Island in New Brunswick and Battra in St. John's are two elegant examples of such domiciles.

In a few cases, individual heritage features stand out, such as Pier 21 in Halifax, or the Tidnish dock and bridge at Tidnish, Nova Scotia.

RAILWAY STRUCTURES

Pier 21

Halifax, Nova Scotia

Deciding to leave their impoverished or dangerous homelands to seek a better life for themselves and their families was often a wrenching choice for immigrants. For many, Canada was the preferred land. Until the 1960s travelling by boat was their only choice. Many arrived in Halifax and would board trains to their final destinations.

In 1928, to facilitate the soaring number of immigrants, the Canadian government constructed a large immigration facility on the waterfront of Halifax to replace the three earlier immigration sheds that had been destroyed by the Halifax explosion a decade before. The new location, known as Pier 21, was adjacent to both the CNR railway station and the comfort of the Nova Scotian Hotel. Trains waited outside the doors for those ready to board.

Between 1928 and 1971, more than one million nervous new Canadians faced interrogation, luggage retrieval, and then finding their train at the Immigration Annex building located on the opposite side of the tracks. During the Second World War, the flow reversed as more than a half million Canadians, most in uniform, passed through Pier 21 to make their way to the ships which would carry them to war. After the conflict ended, Pier 21 witnessed an influx of fifty thousand wives and sweethearts (and twenty-two thousand offspring) of the soldiers, whom they had met overseas.

The flow continued until 1971, when most arrivals began touching down at Canada's major airports, and for two decades the vast building at Pier 21 stood vacant. Finally,

in 1992, work began to convert the site into a memorial museum to tell the story of Canada's immigrants. It opened to the public in 2002. To relate the story to Canada's railways, a railway coach stands outside the main door.

The Pier 21 station annex sits on the opposite side of the road and today houses a brew pub and the offices of a variety of arts organizations. Although comparable facilities in Quebec City no longer stand, Grosse Isle, where thousands were quarantined between 1832 and 1937 over fears of typhoid, retains many early buildings and is now a National Historic Site.

Minister's Island

St. Andrews, New Brunswick

When William Cornelius Van Horne wasn't relaxing in his Montreal mansion or issuing orders from his office in the CPR's Windsor Station, the railway builder might be found enjoying his island home just offshore from St. Andrews by-the-Sea in New Brunswick.

While touring the CPR's newly acquired New Brunswick Railway in 1889, he decided to acquire the island known as Minister's Island. He put his railway's leading architect, Edward Maxwell, to work designing a summer home that Van Horne would call Covenhaven. By the time it was finished, the home contained twenty-six bedrooms, including eleven for guests (most with their own bath), and displayed more than eighty works of art, some created by Van Horne himself. In addition to the mansion itself, two additional buildings stand: the Chateau-style barn with its two towers, also designed by Maxwell, and the circular bath house with its stone pool, now used as the site's iconic image. To reach his summer home, Van

William Cornelius Van Horne liked even his barns built in a Chateau style, such as these structures at his summer estate on Minister's Island, near St. Andrews, New Brunswick.

Horne would ride the CPR's presidential coach to the gravel bar which led to the island where he disembarked from his private car at a gazebo-style station.

Although locals called it Van Horne's island, the "Minister's" name derived from the property's original owner, an Anglican minister. His stone cabin, now vacant, still stands.

Following Van Horne's death in 1915, the home remained in the family until 1941, when his daughter

Adeline died. It then remained in trust until 1961, when the trust sold the property to an American hunter who later decided to subdivide it for seasonal housing. But only two lots were sold and the contents of the mansion went up for auction. Following a public outcry, the province of New Brunswick bought the island and, in 1992, reopened the site for tours. Since 2004 the property has been managed by a non-profit charity that arranges for visits and tours. The building contains

The Battra house in upscale St. John's, Newfoundland, was once home to the Reid family, one-time builders and operators of what was then the Reid Newfoundland Railway.

period furniture and historic displays including a few of Van Horne's own paintings. But visitors need to remember that because of the high tides which cover the gravel bar to the island, there is only a six-hour window to visit and leave the site.

While he was at it, Maxwell designed more than a dozen other homes in St. Andrews, including one for himself, which sits on the mainland side of the sand bar which leads to Minister's Island.

The Van Horne / Shaughnessy House

Montreal, Quebec

While Van Horne's magnificent Montreal mansion was unceremoniously demolished in 1973 amid great public outcry, a second home once occupied by Van Horne was designated a National Historic Site just two years later. The house reflects the opulence of what was then Dorchester Street (now Rene Levesque Boulevard). Designed and built by Thomas Williams in 1874, the limestone duplex rises three storeys and displays a pair of two-storey bays at opposite ends of the building. It is topped with a mansard roof, a style known as Second Empire. The eastern duplex was occupied by Van Horne and later T.G. Shaughnessy, another prominent CPR figure. The west house was originally built for Duncan McIntyre. Threatened with demolition in the 1980s, it was rescued and now houses the reception room and museum of the Canadian Centre for Architecture.

The Battra House

St John's, Newfoundland

The Reid family was to the Newfoundland Railway what Van Horne was to the CPR; even more so, for the family not only built the railway but operated it as well. When they could no longer financially sustain it, they sold the railway to the Newfoundland government in 1923. While the Reids no doubt occupied a number of grand homes, the one most closely associated with the family is the Battra House. The three-storey wooden house was originally designed by architect William Butler for Walter Monroe, who sold it to William Reid, son of Robert Reid the builder of the rail line. Reid lived in the house until 1933 when he sold it to James Hickman. The building remains unaltered on the exterior with its wood cedar roof and leaded glass windows. Inside are seven working fireplaces. The house stands on prestigious Circular Drive in the Rennie Valley National Historic District of St. John's, which also includes the home of the lieutenant governor of the province.

THE CNR SHOPS

Pointe-Saint-Charles

Montreal, Quebec

When the Grand Trunk Railway arrived in Montreal following the opening of the vital Victoria Bridge over the St. Lawrence River, it established an extensive area of maintenance shops in the Pointe-Saint-Charles area. Here, the railroad created massive yards with many of the facilities necessary to build and maintain its growing roster of coaches, freight cars, and steam engines.

An extensive community of railway workers grew around them. The facilities were rebuilt and expanded by the CNR in the 1920s after the new railway company took over the assets of the bankrupt GTR. The shop offices still stand at 1830 Rue Leber, while the shops themselves stretch out behind. The office is a three-storey brick building facing the street, while the massive shops display an Art Deco style common to the period. After the CNR closed the shops, a fire in 2008 caused extensive damage to one of the structures.

Proposals for reuse collapsed, although as of 2014 the AMT (Montreal's commuter rail service) was studying the buildings for storing their suburban trains. The area's heritage value is recognized by Heritage Montreal, which has listed the area on its website as a "threatened emblematic site" and took an active role in public consultations about the site.

There remain in the Pointe-Saint-Charles area a number of other railway related structures, including historic workers' homes on Rue Sebastopol and at the lower end of Rue Congregation. Right at the end of Rue Congregation sit the historic CNR shops.

The CPR Angus Yards

Montreal, Quebec

The CPR's massive Angus yards in the west end of Montreal were among Canada's most productive and famous. More than one thousand newly made steam locomotives puffed out of the Angus shops between 1904 and 1921. The yards extended a kilometre and a half in length and were three quarters of a kilo-metre wide. Amid the sixty-six structures and eighty kilo-metres of track, more than twelve thousand work-ers toiled away. By the time the CPR closed up in 1992, it had moved much of the company's operations to the more distant Saint Luc yards, and the land became more valuable for redevelopment instead. Plans went back and forth between 1993 and 2000, but housing needs prevailed and the yards soon sprouted hundreds of mixed-density homes.

Of the sixty-six railway structures, only four remain. But the area's railway heritage wasn't entirely forgot-ten. The vast locomotive works have been repurposed as a Loblaw's store, the offices refurbished to become more offices, while the former fire hall is now a SAQ (liquor store). Street names, too, reflect the area's rail-way roots, with names like Rue de la Forge, Rue de la Fonderie, Rue de Canadian Pacific, and a street named after the CPR's long serving archivist and chronicler, Omer Lavallée. While a park in the centre of the area is called "Parc des Locomotives," there is not a steam engine in sight. In fact the last of the great steamers, No. 1201, built in 1944, remains in service as a tour train in western Canada.

Newfoundland Railway Yards

St. John's, Newfoundland

The once-extensive yards of the Newfoundland Railway extended west from the station-headquarters building, now the Railway Coastal Museum. Of the other yard structures, only the extensive transhipment warehouse still stands. It is situated on the harbour, east of the station, but has no public access or apparent heritage status. The name of the Newfoundland Railway, however, remains on the entrance above what were once the engine doors.

ICR Blacksmith Shop

Moncton, New Brunswick

It sits on a bleak tract of empty railway lands, across from the equally bleak form of VIA Rail's Moncton station, which is shared with a bus service. It is the lone survivor of a 1906 fire that destroyed much of the ICR's downtown Moncton rail yards. Sitting closer to Albert Street, this boxy brick structure once housed the ICR's blacksmith shop and is a designated heritage feature. While easily visible from the nearby street, it is nonethe-less privately owned and not a public attraction, as such.

The Brass House

Charlottetown, Prince Edward Island

Besides the handsome sandstone station in downtown Charlottetown, Prince Edward Island, another survivor of the town's railway era is known as the Brass House. When the area around it formed part of Charlottetown's large rail yards, the building housed the mechanic's branch of the railway company. Built in 1876, this attractive sandstone structure shows a decorative sculpted rope design above the date stone. Other decorative features on this single-storey building include arched windows. The building, once a visitors' information centre, stands in grassy lawn next to the Founders' Hall. It is not in its architectural grandeur that the building's heritage value lays, but in its age; it is the PEI Railway's oldest surviving structure, and the only yard building that remains.

The Chignecto Ship Railway

Tidnish, Nova Scoita

With such a narrow neck of land, the isthmus of Chignecto, connecting Nova Scotia and New Brunswick, it seemed logical to somehow connect the Bay of Fundy to the St. Lawrence River. While a canal was not feasible in the area, Henry Ketchum concluded in 1875 that a marine railway was the answer. Such a system would lift the ships from one water body, carry them via a railway track, and drop them into the other water body.

Finally, with the financial support of the federal government, Ketchum formed the Chignecto Marine Transport Railway, hired four thousand workers, and got the project started. The route would take the tracks twenty-eight kilometres from Fort Lawrence on the Bay of Fundy to Tidnish Dock on the St. Lawrence. But when the company ran out of money, work stopped and the line remained unfinished. Most of the masonry work was removed over the following years, and much of the route now lies in private hands. However there remains a four-kilometre trail linking the photogenic Tidnish stone arch railway bridge with the remains of the Tidnish Dock Provincial Park. Access is from Highway 366 at Tidnish Bridge, Nova Scotia.

QCR Headquarters

Sherbrooke, Quebec

The Quebec Central Railway was headquartered in Sherbrooke, Quebec. The building that once contained its offices still stands on the town's historic main street, at 179 Wellington Street North. Four storeys high, it is constructed of concrete blocks with "1912" carved into the datestone surrounded by a carved wreath. Double pillars mark the entrance while six pilasters line the façade. The building now houses offices and retail outlets.

The building that housed the ICR ticket office from 1883–1904 survives as 97 Prince William Street in the Trinity Royal Historic District in Saint John, New Brunswick. Although not near the rail lines, the building displays an elegant commercial form with a façade sporting iron pilasters, and Roman arch openings on the third floor windows.

ROUNDHOUSES

This once vital and ubiquitous yard structure posed a difficult challenge to preserve or repurpose. Not only were they generally situated in remote corners of the rail yard, but they had a unique design that was difficult to renovate. Despite those difficulties, there have been many efforts by heritage enthusiasts to save them, usually with little success. One of the most notable failures in eastern Canada came in Kentville, New Brunswick, in 2007 when, despite a public outcry, the town demolished the former DAR roundhouse.

Of the roundhouses that remain, most have been incorporated into other uses. The one-time NTR roundhouse in Napadogan, New Brunswick, has been enlarged to incorporate a veneer plant. The Gibson roundhouse in South Devon, a part of Fredericton, New Brunswick, has been altered to accommodate private businesses. It was built in 1885 to serve Alexander "Boss" Gibson's Northern and Western Railway from Fredericton to Chatham, New Brunswick. A two-stall roundhouse in Cape Tormentine, New Brunswick, sits derelict near the similarly derelict railway station. While the turntable pit remains visible amid tall grasses, the turntable itself has been removed. The New Brunswick and Prince Edward Island rail line reached this point in 1886, but it took until 1914 for the Canadian Government Railways to inaugurate the long-awaited rail-ferry service to Prince Edward Island. The roundhouse and steel water tower reflect the site's significance as a one-time railway terminal.

In Wakefield, Quebec, a turntable was installed to accommodate the Wakefield steam train excursions (now on hold). It was originally located in Kingston, Ontario.

One of the few surviving operational roundhouses is that in the CPR yards at Côte Saint-Luc. This busy facility covers an extensive area in northwestern Montreal. The roundhouse here was erected in 1941, near the end of steam operations, and was one of the last in Canada to be built. The thirty-seven-stall brick structure encircled a thirty-three-metre turntable but has been gradually reduced and now consists of only nine stalls, although the pads from the demolished stalls remain visible, and indeed a few remain in use to store diesel locomotives, as does the turntable.

Vallée-Jonction, south of Quebec City, has remarkably retained an almost complete set of railway structures. In addition to the stone station with a train set on display, and the railway hotel beside the railway bridge, there remains a brick two-stall roundhouse that still displays a turntable. These were built by the QCR and remain part of the railway museum.

However, the best example of a surviving roundhouse in eastern Canada is that in the CNR's Joffre yards at Charny, now part of Levis. This near-complete structure dates to 1881, when the ICR constructed a twenty-four-stall roundhouse. In 1921 the CNR added a further fifteen stalls. Declared a National Historic Site in 1992, the architecture of the building also sets it apart, with decorative cornices and arched window openings, typical of early roundhouses. Although the roundhouse was closed in 1981, it has retained the turntable. Regrettably, despite its status as one of Canada's historic treasures, the CNR will not permit public access. However, images and information is available on the www.historicplaces.ca website.

A few turntable pits remain visible even though the turntables have been removed. One can still be seen in Jonquière's rail yards, another rests in a distant part of the rail yards in Sydney, Nova Scotia.

The Joffre roundhouse in Charny, Quebec, is the largest, oldest, and most historic in eastern Canada. Although it is a designated national historic site, it remains off-limits to all but CN employees. (Photo courtesy Parks Canada.)

CREW HOUSING

Formerly, a key component of most rail terminals were crew bunkhouses. In the early years of railroading, crews usually crammed into converted boxcars, which were small and poorly heated. Beginning around 1895, the YMCA undertook to build much better accommodation at several of Canada's divisional points, but nearly all have since been demolished. Bunkhouses, too, offered improved accommodation. While most of the earliest have gone, a few later structures have survived. A good example still stands in the busy CNR divisional town of Senneterre, Quebec. Situated on Fourteenth Avenue, it is now private housing. The railway's earlier bunkhouse serves as a clubhouse on the town's golf course.

Not all rail lines offered separate accommodation for their section foremen and their families. However, the NTR built two-storey structures from a standard plan for their section workers. As with stations, most have been removed. A few yet linger along the NTR line between La Tuque and Senneterre, often serving today as remote hunting camps or lodges. A good example is the building that now serves as the Duplessis Lodge, located at Mile 34, north of Fitzpatrick. Another is the lodge Chez Hibbard, at Hibbard, and Chez l'Orpailleur.

TUNNELS

In Quebec, a little-known CPR tunnel runs through the massive rock headland upon which Quebec City's ramparts sit. Until the 1950s, CPR steamships sported masts, which were too tall to pass beneath the bridges at Montreal.

As a result, a port facility was constructed at Wolfe's Cove Harbour near Quebec City to transport goods by train. To give their trains a direct link from their main line to the harbour terminal, in 1930 the CPR blasted a 1.5 kilometre tunnel through the rocky mesa. The tunnel rests about 110 metres below the surface. Blasting began at each end in 1930 and the crew met exactly in the middle a year later.

With the opening of the St. Lawrence Seaway in the 1950s, steamships could pass beneath those bridges and began to call at Montreal instead. With the cruise ships bypassing Wolfe's Cove, the CPR converted the site to an intermodal freight terminal, subsequently taken over the Gatineau and Quebec Railway. The tunnel's southern stone arch portal is visible on Boulevard Champlain between the Quebec Bridge and Lower Town Quebec just east of Gilmour Hill, while its northern portal exits the cliff at Dollard-des-Ormeaux-Park on Charest Boulevard.

Prior to the CPR's excavation of the tunnel, the tracks of the NTR occupied the shore from Sainte-Foy near the Quebec Bridge to their station in Lower Town, located where the new ferry terminal now stands.

Tunnels also exist northeast of Port-Daniel on the Chaleur route of VIA Rail (now suspended) and near Shawinigan on VIA Rail's twin train route to Senneterre and Jonquière.

Arguably, the best-known of eastern Canada's railway tunnels is the famous Mount Royal tunnel in Montreal. When the CNoR was vying to gain entry to Montreal, it was originally forced to circumvent to massive volcanic pug know as Mount Royal in order to reach its first station in Montreal's east end. Blasting began at both ends of Mount Royal in 1912 and finished a year later. When the crews met in the middle,

Railway water towers have all but vanished from the landscape. This wood-on-stone CPR tower has been preserved at Dalhousie Station on Quebec's border with Ontario.

they were out of line a mere one inch. The tunnel stretches for five kilometres and lies 188 metres beneath the surface of the mountain.

The CNoR built its tunnel station on the east end where it remained until the 1950s, by which time the CNR had assumed operations of the bankrupt line and Montreal's Central Station had opened. The old station was removed, and the tracks now lie beneath newer development. While the east portal can no longer be seen, the west portal opens out to the Canora AMT station where its limestone entranceway lies close at hand. To avoid the buildup of smoke in the tunnel, the CNoR electrified its line using electric boxcab engines. One of the remaining three original electric boxcabs, built in 1914 and renumbered as CN 6710, sits on display by the modern Deux-Montagnes AMT station. Another is displayed at Exporail, near Montreal. The AMT today uses modern electrified coaches.

WAREHOUSES

Warehouses were often built in conjunction with stations, especially in places where farm produce was being shipped. Only one warehouse has been designated a heritage structure, and that lies in Saint-Quentin, New Brunswick, adjacent to a replica of the original station. This warehouse was built in 1937 of wood shingle siding.

In the Maritimes' prime apple-growing region, the Annapolis Valley of Nova Scotia, several former apple warehouses remain along the route of the former DAR line. Between the 1880s and the 1950s, about 150 apple warehouses were built. Normally measuring fifteen by thirty-five metres, they were capable of filling three fifteen-metre boxcars. The warehouse that remains in Kentville now belongs to the Lions Club. The 1890 warehouse in Canning is now a part of the fire department. The 1908 warehouse in Colebrook is now a Frenchy's clothing outlet. Other historic warehouses remain in Hillaton, Woodville, and Centreville.

In Montreal, the grand Van Horne railway warehouse is designated by Heritage Montreal as a structure of concern. Ten storeys high with decorative features, it was built in 1924 by Duquette and Paternaude and stands on Van Horne Avenue.

While grain elevators were an icon of the western prairies, and a few remain in Ontario, Quebec and the Maritimes were never major grain shippers, so few grain elevators were built. There is one which remains in Tatamagouche, Nova Scotia a few meters from the famous Train Station Inn and dining car restaurant. Another sits beside a freight station on the now-abandoned roadbed of the Canada Atlantic Railway in Lacolle, Quebec.

SUPPORT STRUCTURES

Gone and largely forgotten are the numerous minor structures upon which the railways depended for their operations. Water towers fed the ever-thirsty steam engines and were usually located at every station where there was an adequate supply of water. Only four stand in eastern Canada today. A rusting iron tower rises above the grassy yard area of the former railway terminal of Cape Tormentine, New Brunswick, along with a two-stall roundhouse and the overgrown railway station.

A magnificent water tower stands beside the busy CPR line in Dalhousie Station near the Ontario border. Privately preserved, the red wooden tank rests atop a circular stone base. A pair of more recent water towers have been erected; the one in Wakefield was built in 1984 to supply the popular Wakefield excursion steam train. A hand operated turntable sits here as well, relocated from the CPR yards in Kingston, Ontario. A replica water tower sits near the CNoR Liverpool station in Liverpool, Nova Scotia, where the station has become home of the Hank Snow Home Town Museum.

Many railway structures, once critical, no longer exist. With such advances as grade separation between tracks and roads and improved signalling, road crossing towers are rarely to be found. These were two storeys high, the upper level being the domain of the crossing guard. Two remain. One sits on the grounds of the Sussex Agricultural Museum in New Brunswick, along with a jigger, a wigwag and the little train station from Apohaqui. The crossing tower remained in place on the town's main street until 1960. A second tower rests on its original site on Prince Street in Sydney, Nova Scotia. It is boarded up and the subject of preservation discussions which could mean either its relocation or its demolition.

CELEBRATING THE HERITAGE:
THE RAILWAY MUSEUMS AND DISPLAYS

The loss of Canada's rail lines and passenger service is lamentable, and occasionally unnecessary. Many communities once dependent upon the railways ignore that their rail heritage even exists. Others, however, are determined to celebrate and preserve that heritage by opening museums and assembling heritage railway equipment. Rather than listing in detail all the cabooses that serve as fast food outlets or coaches converted to cabins, this chapter catalogues the more significant preservation efforts.

MUSEUMS OF QUEBEC

ExpoRail: The Canadian Railway Museum

In the southern Montreal suburb of St. Constant, Canadians will find ExpoRail, the country's most extensive collection of historical railway equipment

It all began in March of 1932 with a gathering of railway enthusiasts in Montreal's Chateau Ramezay and the forming of the Canadian Railroad Historical Association. In the following years the group began archiving historical material. In 1950 the association acquired its first piece of rolling stock, an 1892 streetcar from Montreal's streetcar system. As more equipment rolled in, they had to find a place to store it. Happily, in 1960 the Canada Creosoting Company donated a parcel of land in the Montreal suburb of St. Constant, and the CRHA began to realize its long cherished dream of creating a railway museum.

When the Canadian Railway Museum opened in 1965 it could at last show off its growing collection. Twenty-five streetcars, five passenger coaches, and no fewer than twenty steam locomotives were rescued from scrapping in an era when diesel was rapidly replacing steam. As the grounds and the collection grew, more buildings were needed to house the rolling stock, the archives, and a modern visitor centre. In 1970 a flatbed truck hauled in the 1914 station from nearby Barrington. The museum then added a station of its own, known as the Hays Station, named after Charles Melville Hays, the president of the Grand Trunk Railway who perished on the Titanic in 1912. The building came about through a donation from Hays's daughters.

The streamlined Dominion of Canada *is but one of dozens of steam locomotives displayed in Montreal's Exporail, Canada's largest collection of railway rolling stock.*

Today, the collection includes thirty-three steam engines, the oldest of which dates to 1875; eighteen diesel locomotives; twenty-two passenger coaches, two of which date to the 1860s; and forty-three streetcars, ten from Ottawa alone.

Rare for rolling stock, three of the machines are designated National Historical Sites: the private business car belonging to William Cornelius Van Horne, the CPR's first president; a Royal Hudson steam locomotive, CPR No. 2850, one of the engines which carried King George VI and Queen Elizabeth (the Queen Mother) across Canada in 1939 (hence the designation "Royal"); and the CNR's first steam engine, No. 4100.

The museum also boasts a school car, which was a passenger coach fitted as a travelling classroom to serve remote northern communities from the 1920s to the

1960s. Exporail also displays one of the only three remaining Electric boxcabs in Canada (boxcabs were the CNoR built electric engines that travelled through the Mount Royal tunnel). Numbered 6710, it was built for the CNoR in 1914. (The other two are on display at the Deux Montagnes AMT station and at the Canada Museum of Science and Technology.)

Visitors to the grounds may see the equipment housed in the main building and a secondary building, as well as rare railway artifacts. Model railways and miniature train rides will entertain children and adults alike. Visitors can also enjoy streetcar rides, or board a coach at the Hays station for a steam or diesel journey around the property. Bleachers allow spectators to witness the operation of a railway turntable, few of which survive elsewhere.

Musée ferroviaire de Beauce

Vallée-Jonction, a one-time Quebec Central Railway junction on the Chaudière River sixty-eight kilometres southeast of Quebec City in Quebec's Eastern Townships, offers a near complete range of railway heritage in its museum. There is the stone station that sits in the junction, an attractive railway hotel with a mansard roof tower, a truss railway bridge across the river, and a roundhouse built in 1918 with its turntable still in place. To round out the collection, the grounds include a static steam train display. On a siding opposite the station sits steam engine No. 46, built in 1914 for the Grand Trunk Railway. In tow are a tank car, boxcar, and caboose.

It all began in 1990 when a concerned group organized to preserve the station. The following year the federal government designated the station under the

HRSPA. Soon after, the group was welcomed into the Canadian Railway Historical Association, opening the station as a museum in 1994. In 2002 the association obtained the long-sought steam locomotive followed by the boxcar and tank car.

MUSEUMS OF NEW BRUNSWICK

New Brunswick Railway Museum, Hillsborough

For two decades, visitors to eastern New Brunswick could look forward to an excursion on the coaches of the Hillsborough and Salem tourist railway. Formed in 1984 by the New Brunswick division of the CRHA, the trains steamed along an abandoned section of what had been constructed in 1864 as the Salisbury and Harvey Railway, later the Salisbury and Albert Railway. The line crossed ten bridges, including the wooden Hiram Creek trestle. Most of the tours operated in two vintage CN coaches hauled by one of two diesel locomotives or, occasionally, a steam engine.

Despite surviving a deliberately set fire in 1994, the excursions continued along an eighteen-kilometre track until 2004, at which time they were terminated due to insurance issues. Today, of the tracks, the bridges, and the stations, nothing remains. The only record of this ancient railway line left to celebrate is that offered by the New Brunswick Railway Museum. Nonetheless, the collection remains the most impressive in the Maritimes. Stored on the grounds of the replica Hillsborough station, also burned in 1994, the collection includes a 1912 4-6-0 steam locomotive, No. 1009 built in 1912; a pair of diesel locomotives, No. 1754, built 1959, and No. 8245 built 1958; and four passenger coaches, two dating to 1912 and 1911, plus a sleeper and two buffet lounge cars. Other unusual equipment includes a two-way snowplow, a Jordan spreader, and a fire-fighting tank car. In all, the museum collection can claim twenty-six pieces of equipment. A former engine house from a narrow gauge railway plaster operation sits on an adjacent property.

Bristol-Shogomoc Railway Site

In 2000 the CPR's 1914 Florenceville station, a standard single-storey country chalet station, stood empty. The Shogomoc Rail Club moved it to the main street of Bristol to join their three-car collection of CPR coaches. The station now rests on the same site where an identical station was removed in 1971. Here, the three stunningly preserved CPR vintage coaches, built in 1931, include

The Bristol-Shogomoc Railway Site in New Brunswick offers historic displays in the classic CPR station, and fine dining in the CPR coaches.

a former baggage car and two sleeper cars, the *Assiniboine* and the *Grenfell*. They are said to have formed part of the 1939 Royal Tour train. They now offer fine dining and historic displays. Although none are original to the site, they are, nonetheless, listed on the Canadian Registry of Historic Places.

MUSEUMS OF NOVA SCOTIA

Nova Scotia Museum of Industry

Opened in Stellarton in 1995, twenty years after is its original conception, this museum's main mission is to celebrate the province's industrial history, especially as it relates to coal mining where many of Canada's first railways began to operate. Not too surprisingly then, among its railway collection sits Canada's oldest steam locomotive, the *Samson*.

Built in 1838 by the Hackworth Company in in Durham, England, the engine was shipped to Canada to operate at Nova Scotia's Albion Colliery. This unique piece of equipment has a boiler constructed of wood, with the tender and firebox situated on the front of the engine, where the soot and ash would be cleaned by a five-year-old child. Its wheels were in two pieces, so that the outer rim could be removed for repair without having to remove the main part of the wheel from the axel. After operating for more than forty years, it ended up in Chicago, and then the Baltimore and Ohio Railroad museum in Baltimore. From there it went to Halifax and then New Glasgow, finally arriving in the new Stellarton museum in 1993.

At this museum, one can also find Canada's second-oldest steam locomotive, the *Albion*, built in 1840 by the Hackworth Company. It, like its sister, worked the Albion colliery and spent time in the B&O museum before arriving in Stellarton.

Much of the museum's dozen-or-so piece collection of rolling stock, which includes three other steam locomotives, relate to the province's coal mining.

Sydney and Louisbourg Railway Museum

Thanks to dedicated local heritage enthusiasts, the station in Louisbourg, built in 1895 by the Sydney and Louisbourg Railway, was saved from the usual demolition by the railway company. To enhance its heritage value, a small collection of railway equipment was added, including the province's oldest passenger coach, built in 1881. The wooden station itself, built in the Gothic Revival style, features a pair of steep prominent gables on the street side and a large gable by the tracks.

The S&L Railway operated thirty-one steam locomotives on 187 kilometres of track. Its operation was focussed on the Dominion Coal Company, a large conglomerate that had acquired the coal mines and railways between Louisburg and Sydney. Most of the passengers were railway employees. The station closed in 1968 and opened as a museum in 1972. The grounds also include the 1895 freight shed, which offers a model of the area's shipping operations, and a more modern engine house that now serves as a quilt display. Other railway equipment includes a 1914 passenger coach, a boxcar, tank car, and caboose. All other evidence of the S&L Railway has long been removed. Nearby is the massive reconstruction of the French fortress of Louisbourg.

Orangedale Museum

This sole surviving ICR station built in the company's distinctive style was the inspiration for the popular Rankin Family ballad "The Orangedale Whistle." No whistles, however, will emanate from the static display of historic railway equipment beside the station museum. Equipment here includes a 1956 Georgia Pacific diesel locomotive No. 1, a 1955 CNR sleeper car called the *Bonavista*, two boxcars, a flat car, and the much-needed snowplow (a common feature among maritime railway displays). Inside the gangly wooden station are the agent's quarters on the second floor, including kitchen, sitting room, and two bedrooms with original furniture, as well as an archive and model railway display. On the ground floor, the operational displays in the operator's bay include a cipher code book. The men's waiting room is restored to its original appearance while the ladies' waiting room now displays various railway artifacts.

Musquodoboit Railway Museum

The station that houses this museum was built in 1918 when the CNoR was adding to its Maritime collection of branch lines. Passenger service ended in 1960 and the line was abandoned in 1980. The two-storey pyramid-roof station was saved through the efforts of a local school teacher named David Stephens and the area board of trade. It opened as a museum in 1975, adding a display of railway equipment that includes a forty-four-ton diesel engine, No. M563, built for the CNR in 1947; a DAR (CPR) combine car from the province's last mixed train; a flat car; and the usual snowplow. Inside the station are a tourist information centre and a

The popular Tatamagouche Station Inn in Nova Scotia has not only preserved the historic ICR station, but offers accommodation in a fleet of cabooses and dining in a heritage railway coach.

heritage room with historic photos and documents. The former rail bed is now part of a rail trail.

The Train Station Inn

While the Train Station Inn in the seaside town of Tatamagouche is not formally a museum, it is worth a visit and a stay. It began in 1973 when the redundant station was rescued from demolition by eighteen-year-old James Le Fresne. This historic brick ICR station, built in 1889, appears like it belongs in a fairy story with its steeply sloping Gothic roof and high gables. Restorations took place in the 1980s to convert the old building to a bed and breakfast.

The first of seven cabooses began arriving in 1994. They have been converted into suites, a move which required special provincial legislation. The 1928 CNR dining car, No.

7209, in its green, black, and gold trim paint scheme, arrived in 2001 and became the property's main dining facility. And in 2006 the coach gained a partner when the 1905 coach *Alexandra* was placed beside it. This award-winning facility has hosted a governor general and became a setting for the CBC TV movie, *The Day the Women Went.*

DAR Memory Lane Railway Museum

Situated in the restored DAR station, which was built in 1917 to a standard CPR rural station plan, the museum in Middleton features railway memorabilia, photos, artifacts, and even uniforms. A hands-on telegraph key shows how train orders were transmitted along the line. Speeders and an original freight shed, as well as model railways, round out the museum, which operates year-round.

Upper Clements Theme Park

Near the community of Annapolis Royal, the Upper Clements Theme Park, with its many rides and historical buildings, offers a static train display which includes a 4-6-0 former Canadian Northern Railway steam locomotive, No. 1521, dating from 1905, pulling a string of four boxcars built circa 1950, as well as a 1951 wooden caboose.

NEWFOUNDLAND: MUSEUMS OF THE ROCK

The fabled Newfie Bullet passenger train (more properly known as the *Caribou*) that rumbled across Newfoundland ended its last run in 1965. The much-beloved service was replaced by a much faster bus that travelled on the new Trans-Canada Highway. However, much of the Newfoundland Railway's equipment remained and became the focus for a string of railway museums across the province.

Port aux Basques was the line's western terminus, where passengers and freight cars would be transferred onto the ferries bound for North Sydney. It is fitting therefore that beside a replica station, the Southwest Coast Historical Society has assembled a display of railway equipment which includes a 1956 diesel locomotive, No. 934; a pair of tank cars; two baggage cars; and a sleeper car, a boxcar, and caboose, as well as that necessary piece of railway equipment, the snowplow.

In the large west coast mill town of Cornerbrook the Railway Society of Newfoundland has put on display one of the province's most complete and historic train sets, the fabled "Newfie Bullet." "Hauled" by a 1921 4-6-2 steam locomotive, No. 593, the train consists of a baggage car, an express car, a diner and a sleeper, all dating from the 1930–40s, the heyday of the Newfoundland Railway. A plow train with snowplow, a 1956 diesel, a side dump car, and caboose completes the outdoor exhibit. Inside the specially built Humbermouth "station" are displayed photos, telegraph equipment, and a train order semaphore signal box.

The Lewisporte Train Park and Hiking Trail offers, again, a snowplow-led display with a 1952 diesel No. 902, coach and caboose. The station still stands in a separate but original location serving as the Marine Atlantic Office.

Bishop's Falls, a one-time important divisional point on the railway, offers a display that includes a snowplow, a 1956 diesel No. 924, a work car, and caboose. They stand beside the two-storey flat-roofed postwar train station.

Train displays in Newfoundland, such as this in Avondale, typically lead with a snowplow, reflective of the long and snowy winters that bogged down many a train.

Beside the much-refurbished station in Clarenville stand three diesel locomotives dating from the early 1940s to the 1950s, along with a dining car, three flat cars, and a caboose. The site is administered by the Clarenville Historical Society.

Whitbourne was the railway company's most important divisional town between St. John's and Bishop's Falls, and the key junction with the line to the Argentia ferry terminal. The station has been redone to become a municipal office and museum, beside which stands a train display consisting of a snowplow, a 1960 diesel locomotive (No. 940), a 1943 passenger coach, and a caboose. The museum houses photos and videos portraying the railway history of the area. The grounds also contain a monument to those who perished along the line.

On the Brigus branch to Carbonear, the Harbour Grace station, a wooden single-storey structure typical of many stations in the province, is part of the Gordon G. Pike Heritage Railway Museum and Park. Although the building has been maintained in original condition and contains historical artifacts, no equipment is on display. A 1956 diesel (No. 803), however, is displayed beside the similar station in Carbonear.

At the far end of the Bonavista Peninsula, the road-bed of the branch line ends by the *Bonavista* harbour where the former station has been refurbished to become the T.K. Kellway senior centre. Beside the building, a train display includes a 1956 diesel locomotive (No. 932), a dining car, a flat car, and caboose.

One of the island's most distinctive train stations, the Avondale Station Museum, near Conception Bay, also provides a preserved static train display. Headed, naturally enough, by the snowplow, the engine is a 1950 era diesel locomotive (No. 925), and is followed by a baggage kitchen car and 1956 express diner coach, and finally a caboose, and all are sitting on a rare pre-served three kilometre section of Newfoundland's well-known narrow gauge track. Inside displays depict both railway and community history including period furniture in the agent's quarters on the second floor.

Situated in a rural area with a backdrop of mountains, the museum provides the kind of ambience which rail travellers might have enjoyed.

Following the close of the Newfoundland Railway (the CNR, actually) in 1988, the railway's handsome Chateauesque terminal and headquarters in St. John's became home to the Railway Coastal Museum, dedicated in part to the railway heritage of the island. At the original platform, now enclosed, a cross-section of a passenger train circa the early 1940s includes a mail car, coach, galley, dining car, sleeper, and smoker, all with figures in appropriate period costumes. On the track outside the building stands a CNR train set with streamlined diesel (No. 906), a mail car and coach all painted in the CNR's iconic green black and gold paint scheme. The museum also depicts the coastal history of the province plus a model railway layout.

Painted in the classic CNR green-and-gold paint scheme, this train display stands beside the Railway Coastal Museum in St. John's, Newfoundland.

Inside the Railway Coastal Museum, a cross-section of a passenger train shows typical activity inside the train.

PRINCE EDWARD ISLAND

Despite the remarkable number of PEI Railway stations that have managed to survive the demise of the railway, only one has become a museum, the Elmira Railway Museum, in the former eastern railway terminus of Elmira. Most ended up in farmers' fields to serve as various farm buildings, while a smaller number of others have been repurposed as homes or restaurants.

The wooden station at the far eastern railway terminus of Elmira exhibits the railway's standard rural station plan with a wide, hip roof containing a small dormer. Separate doors lead to the waiting rooms while a third door leads to the freight area. The museum displays various artifacts as well as a recreated agent's office and ladies' waiting room complete with pot-bellied stove. A freight shed and small section of track with a speeder complete the display. Located at the terminus of the Confederation Rail Trail, the museum operates seasonally.

At the far western terminus of the former rail line, in the shadow of the Confederation Bridge, the Marine/Rail Heritage Park contains a replica of the Borden station containing an interpretation centre, with a caboose on a short section of rail. The focus of the park, however, is a replica compass that celebrates the rail-ferry heritage of the Carleton-Borden area.

Located near the stunning Kensington field stone station, now preserved as a bar, stands the 1960 CN diesel engine, No. 1762, built in 1960.

The train whistles are silent, the tracks have gone, and travellers now fume in gridlocked traffic. But there is still a way that rail enthusiasts can "hop on board" and follow the ghosts of the old rail lines. They can cross rivers on railway bridges, pause at the stations, and absorb the scenery free of big box stores and numbing asphalt corridors. These are the ghost railways, the abandoned rail lines that far-sighted governments and volunteer groups have made into hiking, cycling, and snowmobile trails.

RAIL TRAILS OF QUEBEC

PPJ, the "Push Pull and Jerk" Trail
Wyman to Waltham

More properly known now as the Cycloparc PPJ, this rail trial passes through the scenic Pontiac region of Quebec, an area west of Aylmer, and has become a popular cycling route between Wyman and Waltham.

The original plan for the Pontiac and Pacific Junction Railway (PPJ) was to link Montreal with Pembroke, Ontario, on the CPR's main route to the west coast (hence "Pacific Junction"). But, short on funding, the rail builders took one look at the expense of crossing the swirling Ottawa River and ended the line at Waltham.

Stations along the line were modest in size, but attractive in style. The standard plan of the Quebec Montreal Ottawa and Occidental (QMO&O), of which the PPJ was part, incorporated a style with steep gabled roofs with extended eaves, and a prominent gable above the centrally situated operator's bay. Of the twenty stations that once lined the route, only two survive. The one in Shawville was modified years ago, and the Pontiac Historical Museum is working to restore the original design. Inside this station/museum are many artifacts which display the heritage of the area. The Luskville station, now relocated to the shore of the Ottawa River, has been sensitively preserved and is a residence.

Waltham served as the western terminal of the abbreviated line with a hotel, roundhouse, and a "Y" for turning the engines. Its original QMO&O style station burned in 1926, after which the CPR, then the line's operator, replaced it with a standard-plan rural station. But that was removed when the trains stopped calling. Where the station once stood, an information kiosk marks the trail head.

From Waltham the trail follows the old rail bed along the scenic shorelines of the Ottawa River and Campbell Lake, passing through villages such as Campbell's Bay, Fort-Coulonge, and the historic streetscapes of Shawville, a rare Anglophone community in Francophone Quebec. This area of gently rolling farmlands mixed with a few rugged outcrops of granite required few railway bridges, although the "black bridge" at the mill village of Davidson is a historic steel truss structure. The trail ends at Wyman, where really nothing stands — no station, no plaques, no facilities of any kind. The right-of-way from this point to near Aylmer is an ATV route. In all, the rail trail extends ninety-two kilometres from Waltham to Wyman and prohibits motorized vehicles.

Prior to the arrival of the PPJ, the Union Forwarding Company ran a small horse-operated portage railway over the three and a half kilometres between the villages of Pontiac and Union Village. This crude track allowed shippers to bypass Chats Falls on the Ottawa River and link steamboat service above and below the falls. The little passenger wagons hosted royalty when in 1869 they carried Prince Arthur around the rapids. Today, only a path through the woods near Union Village serves to remind of the horse railway.

Le P'tit Train du Nord
Saint-Jérôme to Mont-Laurier
Extending two hundred kilometres into the majestic Laurentian Mountains of Quebec, this trail takes its name from the popular ski train that once served the region. The trail itself begins (or ends) at the historic stone former CPR station in downtown Saint-Jérôme, now a suburb of Montreal.

In the 1850s the farmlands of southern Quebec were overcrowded with little land for the farmers to bequeath to their many sons. As a result, concerned parish priests began leading colonization movements to the fertile valleys of the Laurentians. One such cleric, Francois-Xavier-Antoine Labelle, Cure of Saint-Jérôme, began to push for a rail line into the region. The government agreed and the Montreal Northern Colonization Railway was begun, later merging with the QMO&O. In 1882 the CPR assumed the line running trains first from Dalhousie station, then from Viger station, and finally from Windsor Station in Montreal. In 1893 the tracks reached their first terminus which was named Labelle after the line's progenitor. Finally, in 1909 construction halted for good in Mont Laurier, the final terminus of the rail line and today's trail as well.

Ski trains began running in the 1930s as the sport's popularity grew. At its height, the train used eighteen station stops between Saint-Jérôme and Mont-Laurier, the region's most popular ski destination. With the arrival of the auto and improved highways, train service ended in 1981. Soon after, the CPR announced the pending demolition of the attractive little stations along the route. Most of the stations used the standard QMO&O plan, although those at Mont-Rolland, Labelle, and Mont-Laurier were larger two-storey structures, the latter reflecting an common CPR prairie plan. When the original stations needed replacing, the CPR used that line's standard rural plan for stations.

Named for the rail line's early promoter, Father Labelle, the former CPR station in Labelle, Quebec, is a popular stop on the P'tit Train du Nord cycling trail.

Following the abandonment of the line, the municipalities began to lobby for the preservation of their stations, a movement which had its impetus in L'Annonciation when that town's station was threatened. The rail trail was inaugurated in 1996 and has undergone many improvements since then. In particular, several stations have been renovated to serve cyclists. Shuttle buses now operate between Saint-Jérôme and Mont-Laurier, allowing cyclists to cycle in one direction and be chauffeured back to their point of origin.

An archway near the stone CPR station in Saint-Jérôme announces the east end of the route. This end of the trail is, in fact, an urban cycle path where the next several kilometres wind their way through suburban sprawl. Eventually, the trail enters into the more scenic mountainous areas. Stations in Val-Morin and Val-David are replacements of the originals while those in Prévost and Piedmont still bear their QMO&O station style, the former displaying photos of the many stations that lined the route.

One of eastern Canada's last surviving wooden trestles greets users on the P'tit Train du Nord cycling trail as they approach trail's end at Mont Laurier, Quebec.

The Sainte-Adèle station (originally called Mont-Rolland) is a grand two-storey structure hosting a café and a bike rental shop. Sainte-Agathe was one of those rare "witch's hat" stations, with a conical roof atop the waiting room. Although designated as a heritage station under the HRSPA and one of the most interesting stations on the trail, it was torched in 2008. In 2010 the town rebuilt an exact replica, minus a 1913 addition.

Although no longer on the bike trail, the Saint-Jovite station now rests on the town's main street where it has been converted to a popular restaurant. Tracks and a crossing signal enhance the railway ambience of this wonderfully preserved QMO&O station. The nearby Saint-Faustin–Lac-Carré station, also a QMO&O style, does remain on the trail.

The original village of Mont-Tremblant lies on the shore of Lac Mercier, with a main street of heritage structures and the small train station rebuilt in 1998 that contains an art centre. The next in line is the Labelle station. Sheathed in wood shingle siding this 1924 two-storey station contains a popular tavern and information centre. A caboose houses historic displays.

Two identical stations, very close together, lie on the trail in Nominingue and L'Annonciation. Built in 1903 and 1904, respectively, they reflect the CPR's country chalet station plan (single storey, with a wide bellcast roof) and both serve as art galleries and information centres. The station in L'Annonciation displays a plaque recounting the efforts to rescue the stations from the hands of CPR's wrecking crews.

Entering the last station stop in Mont-Laurier, the trail crosses one of the last surviving wooden trestles in eastern Canada. The station itself, now housing the Café de la Gare, was built in 1909 using a two-storey CPR western station plan with hip gable roofs and second floor dormer.

With its proximity to the Montreal area, and the popularity of the Laurentian region, the PTDN trail is one of the most heavily used in eastern Canada. In fact, it now links to Montreal via the Parc Linéaire des Basses-Laurentides cycling trail from Saint-Jérôme to Blainville, a Montreal suburb.

The P'tit Train du Nord trail authority also administers a fifty-eight kilometre rail trail from Morin-Heights to Lac Rémi, known as the "Parc du Corridor Aérobique." It too began as a colonization railway into the Laurentians. Although in parts rougher than the fine stone and asphalt on the PTDN route, is does pass through mountain scenery. The only surviving station is a small wooden structure in the attractive historic farming village of Arundel, relocated a couple of blocks away to serve as a post office, with a display of railway jiggers.

Ligne du Mocassin

Témiscaming to Angliers

Starting at the track-side door of the historic Témiscaming CPR station, the Ligne du Mocassin rail trail follows the Gordon River for 6.7 kilometres through this attractive "garden city" mill town as a paved walking and cycling trial before converting to a rougher stone dust ATV and snowmobile trail at the eastern end of town. As it makes its way through the former mill village of Lumsden, a short distance east, it passes a blue VIA coach now serving as a Subway restaurant. Beside the eatery, a replica CPR chalet station painted in the original yellow and red colour scheme houses an ice cream parlour.

The snowmobile and ATV trail continues to Ville-Marie where it follows the right-of-way of the line for forty-five kilometres from Ville-Marie to the trail's end at Angliers. This portion of the trail is reserved for non-motorized travellers during the spring and summer months.

Sadly, outside of that grand station in Témiscaming, no railway structures have survived on the line. A photo gallery in the station shows images of nearly all the line's stations. However, an interesting railway related display awaits at Angliers, where logs were transported by tug to the waiting trains. A boxcar marks the end of the trail, while the former logging warehouse of the Compagnie Internationale du Papier (CIP) marks the original end of rail itself and the location of the town's small wooden station. Now a museum, the warehouse displays photos and videos of the area's logging history. The historic tug *T.E. Draper* is open for tourists beside the CIP warehouse.

Route des Draveurs: Gatineau Valley Linear Park

Low to Maniwaki

It seems odd that a seventy-kilometre rail trail would be named after the area's historic log drivers (*draveurs* who plied the turbulent nearby Gatineau River). This trail follows the former roadbed of the Ottawa and Gatineau Valley Railway between Low and Maniwaki, north of the Gatineau Park area near Ottawa.

The OGVR was opened to Maniwaki from Hull in 1903. Along the line, stations were close together, most of them incorporating the standard QMO&O storey-and-a-half plan with extended steep gable roofs. When the old QMO&O stations burned or needed replacing, the CPR, the lessee, would use their standard single-storey hip-roof station plan. As is usual with the CPR, nearly every station was removed. The rare exceptions are the ones in Wakefield, which is now a restaurant, and in Venosta, where the historic QMO&O station, now a residence, remains on site by the trail. Happily, it retains most of its exterior architectural features along with a freight shed, well, and station outhouse. Others now sit in various private locations around the region. (One such small CPR station is visible from Highway 105 at Cross Loop Road.)

The northern terminus of the trail is in Maniwaki near the original site of the station and yards. From the town, the coarse stone trail winds through wooded areas and into the village of Messines. Southward, it passes by the summer homes of Blue Sea Lake. Then come the hills and woodlands of Clemow. The route then swings into Gracefield, passing behind the main street. From here it crosses through farm country and then back into the woods. At Venosta the trail encounters the only piece of actual railway heritage en route, the original QMO&O station. The south end of the rail trail ends at Low, only a few kilometres from the village of Wakefield, the terminus of the Wakefield Steam Train. Here, near the 1929 CPR train station, a turntable and water tower have been built to accommodate the steam excursions. (At this writing, the excursions were in question due to the costs involved in repairing damage from landslides along the track.)

Vélopiste Jacques-Cartier/Portneuf

Valcartier to Rivière-à-Pierre

From the sprawling outskirts of Quebec City, this sixty-eight-kilometre rail trail follows the route of the National Transcontinental Railway initiated by Prime Minister Wilfred Laurier. The stone dust trail (cyclists only) begins at Saint-Gabriel-de-Valcartier making its way through fertile farmlands (and suburban sprawl) and into the Laurentian Mountains and the railway town of Rivière-à-Pierre where it meets the Quebec and Lac-Saint-Jean Railway, an 1880 route, now part of the CNR system.

Work on organizing a rail trail began within a year of the CN vacating the route, and by 1997 the trail was completed to Saint-Léonard, and had made it

A genuine piece of railway heritage is found in Venosta, Quebec, where a rare QMO&O-style station yet survives on site along the Véloroute des Draveurs rail trail.

to Rivière-à-Pierre a year later. The trail passes over a few small bridges, such as those over the Ontaritze and Sainte-Anne Rivers on a pair single-span Howe truss structures. A large trail-side parking area in the busy town of Saint-Raymond displays a historic plaque which recounts the history of the area and includes a 1920 photograph of the inelegant town station.

Although it is called Duchesnay Station, this resort hotel complex through which the trail passes began life as a government forestry camp and operated from 1933 until 1999, when it became a SEPAQ (Société des établissements de plein air du Québec).

The trail then winds through more mountainous terrain near Saint-Léonard, ending at "La Terminus" of Rivière-à-Pierre, a kilometre or so from the VIA Rail station. This intriguing and nicely landscaped parking area includes a map and picnic tables of granite, a material for which the region is famous. As long as service to the VIA station continues, cyclists may load their bikes onto or off the train and enjoy a double dose of the region's rail heritage.

Velopiste Bellechasse
Armagh to Levis

The Bellechasse rail trail follows the roadbeds of the former NTR and the Quebec Central Railway for seventy-four kilometres, from Armagh for to Saint-Henri on the outskirts of Levis. The eastern portion of the route from Armagh to Saint-Anselme follows the NTR built between 1909 and 1913. In 1915, to commemorate the death of Frederick Monk, a former Canadian minister of transport, the line was named the Monk line. The original NTR line had made its way northwest from Edmunston and then cut westerly well to the south of the Grand Trunk, which followed the St. Lawrence River, before the two lines linked near Levis. In 1987 the CNR rerouted its line to more directly link with the CNR west of Rivière-du-Loup on its main line, thereby abandoning the redundant Monk line.

In 2008 eight municipalities initiated a rail trail which would incorporate both the abandoned Monk line as well as an abandoned section of the Quebec Central Railway. Much of the terrain through which it passes between Armagh and Saint-Malachie is farmland dotted with historic villages. At Saint-Malachie it crosses the Etchemin River and follows its banks passing the picturesque riverside community of Saint-Anselme, south of which it connects with the roadbed of the QCR. It terminates at Saint-Henri near Levis. Parking and food can be found in the towns and villages on the way, although no significant railway structures appear along the trail. However, of the eleven stations built on this route, four do survive, though they have been moved. The station at Saint-Anselme, a two-storey pyramid roof style, and at Saint-Malachie, a storey-and-a-half NTR style with dormers in the hipped roofline, are nicely preserved as a residences.

The Petit Témis RailTrail
Edmunston, New Brunswick, to Rivière-du-Loup

This 135-kilometre cycling trail, one of eastern Canada's most scenic, follows the roadbed of the Temiscouata Railway (later the CNR) from a point north of Edmunston to the outskirts of Rivière-du-Loup. Much of the route follows the shores of Lac Temiscouata and the Madawaska River, making for a pleasant waterside trail. It is touted for being an interprovincial trail passing through both Quebec and New Brunswick. The St. Lawrence and Temiscouata Railway, as it was then called, was in 1886, to link Rivière-du-Loup on the Intercolonial Railway with Edmunston. The portion of the track north of Cabano was abandoned in 1983, south of that to Edmunston, in 1989.

In addition to the ample rest stops and camping grounds, this paved rail trail can claim two on-site historic stations. The one at Degelis is a storey-and-a-half wooden structure with wide sloping roof and now houses an art gallery, café, and tourist information office known as "la gare de l'heritage." The spacious grounds contain several picnic tables. A bit further north, the trail encounters the Cabano station. Stations of this style are rare across Canada. The two-storey red wooden station has decorative window frames and is well preserved on the outside. Inside

The former GTR station in Lyster, Quebec, was brought back to its original site to serve cyclists and hikers on the rail trail.

it contains a popular bed and breakfast, a trail-side pleasure for weary cyclists. It was built in 1889 by the St. Lawrence and Temiscouata Railway and is listed on the Canadian Registry of Historic Places.

A two-span Howe truss bridge carries the trail over the Madawaska River, the only bridge of note on the route. The trail's termini lie at Chemin Fraserville in Rivière-du-Loup and at the Pavillon de l'Estacade in Edmunston.

Parc Lineaire de Lotbiniere / Bois Francs

Levis to Richmond

This may qualify as one of eastern Canada's more historic rail trails as it encompasses the Grand Trunk's original Levis to Montreal route. Built in 1854, originally between Levis and Richmond, it was part of the plan to link Canada's colonies from Rivière-du-Loup, where it met the Intercolonial Railway, through Montreal and on to Toronto and Sarnia. In 1898, as part of its overall upgrading, the GTR bypassed the original routing with a newer and more direct route further north between Levis and Saint-Hyacinthe. Both routes operated until 1989 when the CNR abandoned the older route.

Most of the rail trail is flat and straight, crossing the St. Lawrence lowlands' most fertile farmlands. The eastern portion, called the Lotbinière Trail, runs seventy-seven kilometres from Levis to Dosquet. The western segment, the Bois Francs Trail, continues a further 57.5 kilometres from Dosquet to Victoriaville. It makes its way through historic francophone villages like Saint-Agapit, Dosquet, Lyster, and Warwick.

Stations have survived in Saint-Agapit, where the wooden single-storey, hip-roof station offers historical information. At Lyster the similar, but somewhat larger station was rescued from a private property in 2004 and returned to its original site to accommodate cyclists with historic plaques and benches for the weary traveller. In downtown Victoriaville a "faux" station, built to resemble traditional stations, offers information and washrooms for cyclists.

Warwick station, attractively restored, rests on its original site in the core of the community. From Warwick the route continues through farm country entering the quiet village of Danville where a string of former railway hotels line Rue du Depot opposite the now vacant station grounds. There is parking for cyclists in Danville. The trail then makes its way to Richmond where it parallels existing tracks to the large brick station which has been repurposed as a restaurant and motel, fenced off from the busy yards beside it.

Other Quebec Trails

Quebec's many abandoned rail lines have resulted in a dense network of shorter rail trails, such as the Route des Champs, a thirty-six kilometre trail between Marieville and Granby. The Tomifobia Trail follows the route of the former Massawippi Valley Railway, which originally linked Newport, Vermont, with Lennoxvile, Quebec. The line was abandoned by the CPR (then the operator) in 1990, and in 1993 became the Tomifobia Nature Trail running nineteen kilometres between Beebe on the U.S. border and Ayers Cliff. Stations in both places still stand, though both are residences. Along the route, an 1895 train accident, which killed both the engineer and conductor when a boulder fell onto the tracks, is commemorated with an inscription on the very boulder, as well as a memorial marker.

The Estriade Trail traces the route of the Central Vermont Railway, built in 1859–61, from the outskirts of the busy divisional town of Farnham (although a more fitting starting point is across from the current station where a diesel is on display), across farmlands and around wooded hills to a picturesque lakeside stop in Granby, where a replica of the original station houses a MacDonald's restaurant and bike rental shop. The trail continues along the CVR to Waterloo, where it follows municipal streets to pick up the former Southeastern Railway, built from Richford, Vermont, to Drummondville in 1878 (later taken over by the CPR). At its junction with the former GTR (still an active CNR line) it passes the remarkable towered Acton Vale station before ending near Drummondville. Both rail operations were abandoned in 1989 and the trail inaugurated soon afterwards.

RAIL TRAILS OF NEW BRUNSWICK

New Brunswick maintains, often in conjunction with the Trans-Canada Trail, a series of trails, many of which follow abandoned sections of rail line. Trail users can thank the benevolence of the Irving Corporation, which turned 377 kilometres of abandoned rail line over to the province.

A sixty-nine-kilometre section runs from East Bathurst, crossing the water at Inkerman on a long trestle, before ending at Tracadie, with segments passing through Caraquet, Lamaque, and Shippagan. It follows the tracks of the Caraquet Railway, built in 1888, from the ICR at Gloucester Junction.

The Tantramar Trail, which begins at the Tantramar High School in Sackville, leads through Port Elgin to Cape Tormentine, once the terminal for ferry service to Prince Edward Island and where the station, roundhouse, and water tank survive, despite being ignored and neglected. The line was established in 1886 as the New Brunswick and PEI Railway although railway ferry service didn't start until 1917.

A Trail Visitor Centre in the South Devon neighbourhood of Fredericton, a building which has been designed to resemble the old CNR South Devon station, marks the start of a number of rail trails. Originally called Gibson, this railway town included freight yards, machine shops, and a roundhouse, which still stands beside the Bill Thorpe walking bridge. From the centre the Nashwaak Trail follows the abandoned CN railway roadbed northward along the Nashwaak River for 7.5 kilometres to the abandoned Penniac CN railway bridge. From there it continues to the Nashwaak Bridge. The line was the creation of Alexander "Boss" Gibson in the 1880s, who also established a cotton factory, one of the largest in Canada, in Marysville. That community, through which the trail passes, was Gibson's company town for his mill workers. Today the workers' brick tenements, some Gibson family homes, and the massive repurposed mill form a designated heritage district, one worth exploring. CN abandoned the line in 1995.

From the centre a rail trail also leads west, paralleling the river. It is paved until it reaches the western end of town, where it then becomes stone-dust track. Here, it passes by the unusual two-storey wooden station at Burtts Corner, continuing through Millville, and ending at Woodstock. It began life as the New Brunswick Railway in 1873 and ended life as part of the CPR in the late 1990s.

From Woodstock, once a key rail junction, the trail crosses the St. John River on an imposing four-span Howe truss bridge on its way to Hartland and the world's longest covered bridge. At Bristol the restored CPR station from Florenceville is the focus for the Bristol–Shogomoc Rail Site which includes a fine dining restaurant in a pair of vintage CPR coaches. From Perth-Andover, devastated by floods in 2010, the route continues a short distance on to Aroostook Junction, which was once a major rail junction with housing, roundhouse, and a station, which sits overgrown by the trail. A short distance beyond, the trail crosses the Aroostook River on a rare curving steel span bridge. After passing through Grand Falls, where a small boxcar shaped CPR station sits vacant by the trail, the trail ends at the north end of the town. From Perth-Andover a branch extends from the opposite side of the river to its terminus at Plaster Rock.

South of the centre the trail crosses the St. John River on the 581-metre Bill Thorpe Walking Bridge, the longest of its kind in the world. In historic Fredericton, the trail links to the former CPR line and, as the Crosstown trail leads to the refurbished CPR station. The trail makes its way west of the city becoming the Valley Trail before ending a short distance further.

NOVA SCOTIA'S RAIL TRAILS

Nova Scotia's trail system has evolved on two main rail corridors, that of the Dominion Atlantic Railway, built between Windsor Junction and Yarmouth, and the Halifax and Southwestern Railway, which ran between Halifax and Yarmouth. The former, built between 1869 and 1879 became part of the vast CPR empire, which abandoned the line in 1990. The latter was taken over by the Canadian Northern Railway (which built many of the line's stations) before being assumed by the CNR, which abandoned the line in 1988. A branch line of the ICR connected Pugwash with Pictou in 1890, and was abandoned by the CNR in 1986.

St. Margaret's Bay and Shelburne County Trails

The St. Margaret's Bay Trail follows thirty-three kilometres of the CNoR route from Hubley to Hubbards, where a replica of the old CNoR station stands at the intersection of Routes 3 and 329. The CNoR station at French village, however, is an original station and contains a bike rental shop and café. From there, the trail continues to follow the rail bed to Chester, where it encounters a CNoR class 2 station, now a tourist centre and museum. An identical style of CNoR station in Liverpool is now the Hank Snow Home Town Museum. There is a break in the rail trail through Liverpool before it becomes the Shelburne Rail Trail. Much of the route between Liverpool and Pubnico is a rough surface that is a challenge for cyclists. The going gets easier at Pubnico, where new stone dust has been put down. The route follows Water Street to the ferry terminal in Yarmouth, although no heritage railway structures remain here.

The Evangeline Trail

Nova Scotia's "Evangeline Trail" can scarcely be called a true rail trail, since much of the former rail bed is discontinuous and in poor shape. It does, however, link a string of heritage features related to the DAR and are described in chapter 6.

TransCanada Trail

Pugwash to Pictou

This rail trail is both scenic and historic, and suitable for non-motorized use. The Intercolonial Railway was one of the earliest rail operations in Nova Scotia, having built a line in 1890 from Oxford Junction to Pictou Landing, with a short branch line to Pugwash. From Pictou Landing a ferry service operated to Georgetown on the PEI Railway. The CNR abandoned the branch in 1986, and the route was converted to a rail trail.

This stone-and-dust trail leads from the small railway hamlet of Oxford Junction through the town of

Oxford into Pugwash, where the steep-roofed brick station is now a library. From Pugwash Junction the route follows the shore to Tatamagouche, where a similar brick station has been converted to the popular Station Inn bed and breakfast, with a string of cabooses serving as suites with fine dining available in a CPR coach. The trail leaves Tatamagouche crossing a single-truss bridge, and swings inland for several kilometres before crossing the Wallace River trestle, the trail's longest, on a series of truss spans perched on stone piers. The trail doesn't make it quite as far as the grand seaside Pictou station, but a few blocks on the town's historic streets completes the journey.

PRINCE EDWARD ISLAND'S CONFEDERATION TRAIL

Construction on the PEI Railway began in 1870, but five years would pass before the line opened. A vast improvement over the red mud roads that bogged down wagons and buggies, every town and village lobbied for a station, resulting in a winding route with stations roughly every four kilometres. The main line stretched 273 kilometres, from Tignish in the west to Elmira in the east, while branch lines fed Charlottetown, Georgetown, Souris, and Montague. Ferry service connected the PEIR to the mainland, from Summerside to Shediac, and from Georgetown to Pictou until 1917 when the crossing shifted to Borden–Cape Tormentine. While stations at the ferry terminals were decidedly grander, the local stops were usually simple wooden structures, with some notable exceptions.

Abandonment by the CNR began in 1984, and within five years Prince Edward Island no longer had a railway. But today's Confederation Trail has taken over the roadbeds and converted them to paved and stone-and-dust bicycle paths, ideal for enjoying the pastoral countryside and ocean views of Canada's smallest province.

An appropriate starting point would be the Joe Ghiz (a former premier) Memorial Park, not far from Charlottetown's historic red stone station. Royalty Junction allows trail users to choose an easterly or westerly course to follow. Numerous parkettes and parking areas line the route, as do heritage stations.

To the west, the route passes stations at Kensington, a designated heritage station constructed of field stones and now a bar; Summerside's two-storey station, which houses a regional library; Emerald Junction, which is now a residence; O'Leary, now a café; and Alberton, a field-stone structure now a tourist office. A replica station marks the one-time ferry terminal of Borden.

Heading east, the Confederation Trail splits into three trails that follow three old branch lines. One leads to Georgetown, where a replica station reflects the original structure with its decorative tower. A second branch makes its way to Cardigan before ending at Montague, where the wooden station now houses a gift shop and information centre. A third branch leads past the Merrill station, which reflects the standard plan used by the rail line, and ends in Elmira, where the small wooden now houses the Elmira Railway Museum.

NEWFOUNDLAND TRAIL PROVINCIAL PARK

Seven years after the last of the rails were sent off to South America in 1990, Newfoundland established the T'Railway Provincial Park, a linear rail trail that follows the former rail line 888 kilometres across the province from Port aux Basques to St John's. Bridges and trails are maintained by the T'Railway council, although only those portions in or near urban areas are suited for cycling — such as the 11 kilometres section between St. John's and Donovans and the 4.3 kilometre stretch at Corner Brook. For the most part, the trail is popular primarily with equestrians, cross-country skiers, snowmobilers, and ATV users. A portion east of Corner Brook now lies beneath the asphalt of the Trans-Canada Highway, which in many areas runs parallel to the trail. It is a constant struggle to keep the many bridges in a sufficient state of repair to allow safe use. Of the 130 bridges, only the 282-metre four-span truss bridge across the Exploits River is of any great size. Happily, it has been resurfaced and is suitable for walking and cycling.

A few stations have survived in larger communities having been repurposed. The most interesting of these is the ancient wooden station, perched on a hillside, in Avondale. This mansard-roof structure began life in 1888 as a telegraph station. It has been refurbished and repainted and now hosts a seasonal museum and train display. Other trail side stations include Bishop's Falls, Clarenville, Deer Lake, Glenwood, and Whitbourne, which was once one of the rail line's most important inland towns. All have been repurposed save the station at Glenwood, which awaits a new life as a possible museum. Smaller, more remote stations have managed to hang around, such as those at Heatherton (now boarded up), and Spring Brook, (now a private cabin).

The trail presents ample wilderness and spectacular mountainous terrain, such as near the four Gaff Topsails hills, and ocean views, where during the spring glittering icebergs float into view on the eastern segments. Various remote inland portions serve as crude roads for Newfoundlanders to access cabin and cottage locations along the trail. Sadly, despite the ongoing struggles to maintain such a long trail in remote locations, trail users have lamented the extensive and unsightly clear-cut logging along many western and central sections of the trail, and the damaging use by logging trucks.

The eastern terminus of the trail lies beside the train display at the St. John's Railway Coastal Museum located in the elegant Chateauesque station.

ALL ABOARD: TRAIN TRIPS YOU CAN STILL ENJOY

With the arrival of the auto age and the disinterest of various levels of government in rail travel, rail passenger service has lost its former dominance. Despite this regrettable decline, there remain some opportunities to relive and celebrate this vital period in eastern Canada's history. While previous tour train operations have not enjoyed great success in Quebec and the Maritimes, new ventures offer opportunities to enjoy the comfort and scenery from a passenger seat. VIA Rail provides services both scenic and vital across the area, though diminished from previous levels.

Train le Massif de Charlevoix

Quebec City

This train trip rivals anything Canada's western tour-train operations can offer. Launched in 2011, the Train le Massif de Charlevoix hugs the St. Lawrence River — the vast riverine expanse on one side and the looming cliffs of le Massif on the other. The route extends between the stunning Montmorency Falls and La Malbaie. Travel options include a return trip from the Falls to Baie-Saint-Paul, or from Baie-Saint-Paul to La Malbaie. The full journey takes in everything between the falls and La Malbaie.

After inching away from the new station beneath the foaming falls, the modern luxury coaches follow a 140-kilometre route, taking in the magnificent Sainte-Anne-de-Beaupré basilica, built in 1928 and now a pilgrimage site, and the picturesque village of Saint-Joachim, with its seventy-four metre waterfall, before plunging through a train tunnel at Les Caps.

Those stopping at Baie-Saint-Paul can can stroll its gallery-filled streets or visit the luxurious Hôtel La Ferme. The full excursion terminates at La Malbaie, where travellers may arrange a visit to the historic Fairmont Manoir Richelieu or stroll Chemin des Falaises or the Rue du Quai in Pointe-au-Pic.

Besides the day trips, four-course sunset dinner excursions offer meals created by the renowned chefs from Le Fairmont Manoir Richelieu Hotel.

Trains depart from the base of the world famous Montmorency Falls, where a modern station and gift shop are situated. The site also accesses Montmorency Falls Park.

Guests prepare to board the Train de la Massif Charlevoix near Quebec City to experience some the grandest trackside scenery in eastern Canada as it glides along the St. Lawrence River and beneath the looming cliffs of le Massif de Charlevoix.

The Ameril Train

Gaspé, Quebec

The newest of the tourist routes in Quebec is the Ameril Tour Train. Using three new coaches equipped with table seating, the train offers runs from Carlisle to Bonaventure, from Gaspé to Percé, and Gaspé to L'Anse-à-Beaufils, the last two routes linking with cruise ships that call in at the port of Gaspé. The route goes though mountains and along the water's edge, crossing the stunning high bridge at L'Anse-à-Beaufils.

Le Réseau Charlevoix

La Malbaie, Quebec

Another newcomer to the tour-train scene is the Réseau Charlevoix. The regional municipality of Charlevoix, situated on the St. Lawrence River northeast of Quebec City, has put together a transportation network consisting of both bus and rail travel. Operating between June and October, the self-contained, two-unit rail cars shuttle between Baie-Saint-Paul and La Malbaie on its eastern leg, a journey of about eighty minutes, with stops at Les Éboulements and Saint-Irénée. The western shuttle operates from December through April, and travels between Baie-Saint-Paul and Grand Point, and lasts about forty minutes. While the coaches offer no onboard amenities, the scenic route squeezes between the looming Charlevoix cliffs and the wide St. Lawrence. The Baie-Saint-Paul station lies near the popular new La Ferme luxury hotel.

The Orford Express
Sherbrooke, Quebec

This elegant refurbished train departs the historic CPR station in Sherbrooke, Quebec, for the bucolic lakeside setting of Magog, as well as the community of Eastman. Its three chrome coaches are able to seat more than two hundred diners. Each coach has its own kitchen. Three meal options are available, as well as an overnight stay in Magog or a cruise on Lake Memphremagog.

Most departures take place Thursdays through Sundays. On Wednesdays, the tour runs between Magog and Bromont. The trip lasts about three to four hours and rumbles across steel bridges while offering vistas of scenic Lake Memphremagog and Orford Lake. There is also a twenty-minute stop beside the lake at Magog. Onboard entertainment may be a local folk singer or, at Christmas, a visit from Père Noël. The operation was

launched in 2006 and follows a small section of the former CPR Short Line, which linked Montreal to Saint John, New Brunswick. VIA Rail ended its own service on the line in 1994. (A fire in 2014 forced the company to cancel its operations for that year.)

Wilderness Adventures
Laurentian Mountains, Quebec

VIA Rail offers scheduled train services into the wilderness of Quebec's fabled Laurentian Mountains. On alternate mornings, two trains are hooked together to depart the Gare Centrale in downtown Montreal. The train circumnavigates Montreal Island, picking up passengers at suburban stations in Ahuntsic and Pointe-aux-Trembles. Escaping Montreal's sprawling suburbs, the train crosses a pair of long trestles over the St. Lawrence and enters the fertile St. Lawrence farmlands as it makes its way toward to the looming Laurentian Mountains. Just before entering Shawinigan, it crosses the high trestle above the Sainte-Ursule Falls. The mightier of the two trestles actually crosses a river left dry by an earthquake in the seventeenth century, before a lesser trestle crosses the falls themselves.

After stops at the historic stations in Joliette and Shawinigan, the train halts at the country station of Hervey-Jonction, where the two train sections split, the *Saguenay* lurching northeast toward Jonquière to follow the former tracks of the CNoR, while the *Abitibi* makes its way along the route of the NTR to Senneterre. Both sets of tracks today are owned by CN Rail.

Both routes showcase the lakes and forests and remote communities of the forested mountains. The shorter of the two routes is the *Sagueney*. It stops in villages

VIA Rail's Abitibi *and* Saguenay *trains reunite at Hervey-Jonction after winding through the wilderness of northern Quebec.*

like Rivière-à-Pierre and Lac-Édouard, with its classic CNoR station. After it passes hunt camps like Triton and Summit, the train emerges from the hills to begin its scenic descent to Lac-Saint-Jean and the stations at Chambord and Hébertville. The Jonquière station is a modernistic combined bus and rail terminal. Trains originally continued on to the Chicoutimi station, which is now a mall and office complex.

The Lac-Saint-Jean region was opened up with the arrival of the colonization railway, but prosperity was due to the plentiful hydro power and deep water access for bauxite boats, which attracted aluminum smelters like Alcan.

But the longer and more interesting of the two journeys is that which heads to Senneterre, passing through remote towns and villages whose only link to the outside is the train. Between Hervey-Jonction and La Tuque the train crosses the Rivière du Milieu on the highest trestle in Quebec still used by passenger trains. The last road-accessible community is the mill town of La Tuque, and then it's along the Saint-Maurice River towards several hunting and fishing camps some of them, such as the Duplessis camp, using the former section houses of the NTR railway.

Mountains eventually give way to flat, sandy forest lands and the town of Parent. Despite having a population of over seven hundred, it lacks road access, and still depends heavily on its historic rail links. Along with its CN Rail marshalling yard (it was originally a NTR divisional point) the town's main industries include the Industries Parent sawmill, which took over the assets of the former Kruger mill, and snowmobile tourism. This journey ends in the early evening at the busy railway town of Senneterre. With its extensive yards and maintenance buildings it is still a divisional point with a postwar two-storey station.

by suburban sprawl for the last several kilometres into Montreal. Most trains stop at the heritage stations in Drummondville and Saint-Hyacinthe.

The *Ocean Ltd.,* which runs between Montreal and Halifax, offers fine views along its route between Halifax and Matapédia with stops at the grand historic ICR stations at Amherst and Sackville and the more modest country station at Rogersville. Regrettably, the portion of the route from Matapédia to Montreal is a night-train, preventing travellers from enjoying views along the Matapédia River Valley and across the St. Lawrence River, nor will they see the historic stations situated there, such as those at Rimouski, Trois-Pistoles, La Pocatière, Saint-Pascal, and Montmagny.

Some of Halifax's more significant sites lie but a short distance from the VIA station. The elegant neoclassical Halifax station is connected to the luxurious and historic Westin Nova Scotian Hotel, while the Pier 21 National Historic Site, which documents Canada's compelling immigrant story, is a block from the station.

The Quebec South Shore

The Quebec segment of VIA Rail's Quebec–Windsor corridor route is always worth a trip. Several daily trains operate between Quebec City and Montreal, crossing two of Canada's most spectacular railway bridges over the swirling St. Lawrence River as they do — the cantilever bridge from Quebec City to Charny, and the Victoria Bridge into Montreal. VIA's castle-like Gare du Palais station in Quebec City is worth arriving early for. Apart from the bridge crossings, the scenery between the two cities is largely uninteresting and dominated

Quebec North Shore and Labrador Railway

Sept-Îles , Quebec

Although this rail line operates a scheduled passenger train service, it is not part of VIA Rail's dwindling network. Rather, its main role was to connect the port of Sept-Îles with the iron mines of Schefferville, Wabush, and Labrador City. Construction began in 1950 and took four years to complete due to harsh terrain and even harsher weather. This 350-kilometre journey lasts a full day, but takes the traveller through some of eastern Canada's most rugged terrain.

Within the first couple of hours after departing the Quonset hut style station in Sept-Îles, the train, which consists of up to six coaches (including a restaurant car), rumbles through a 650-metre tunnel, soars above the Moisie River on a 275-metre trestle, and snakes along hillsides 200 metres above the valleys below. Stops en route are often for hunters and fishermen, while other travellers continue on toward Emeril Junction and a connection to Labrador City. North of this point, the train enters an area of stunted trees and flat sand plains before arriving at the rugged northern town of Schefferville.

Since 2005 all passenger service is provided by the Tshiuetin Rail Transportation Inc. (TRT), the only railway in Canada owned by the First Nations. The group owns outright the tracks and freight service between Emeril Junction and Schefferville, while the QNS&L focusses on shipping iron ore products to Sept-Îles from Labrador City where the Iron Ore Company of Canada processes its ore. Stations along this route were not constructed for their architecture elegance, but rather for simple utility, although Sept-Îles station, where the QNS&L is headquartered, displays a pair of steam locomotives. The TRT operates two weekly return trips.

Montreal's Commuter Rail Heritage

Travelling on commuter trains seems like almost the last type of excursion which would reward a heritage rail enthusiast. However, the AMT (Agence métropolitaine de transport) commuter service in and out of Montreal's Gare Centrale provides both history and scenery from their frequent trips.

Stunning views of the mighty St. Lawrence River spread out when the trains traverse the many bridges onto Montreal Island. These include the Sainte-Anne Bridge across the Ottawa River, the Victoria Bridge, and the LaSalle Bridge. The LaSalle route also passes the historic wooden LaSalle commuter station. Two bridges lead to the commuter station at Deux-Montagnes where one of the last of the CNoR's 1914 boxcab electric units that once operated on this line is displayed adjacent to the modern station. This route also carries its passengers through the historic Mount Royal tunnel and on to the Mount Royal station, which now serves as a restaurant that is the focus of this historic railway town.

Station lovers will enjoy the commuter route to Vaudrieul with historic CPR stations situated at Montreal West, Beaconsfield, Valois, and Dorion. Trains no longer stop at the boarded up Westmount station although its architectural elegance may yet be visible behind the shrubs which obscure the trackside façade.

BIBLIOGRAPHY

BOOKS AND ARTICLES

Adair, Daryl T. *Canadian Rail Travel Guide*. Markham, ON: Fitzhenry and Whiteside, 2004.

Andreae, Christopher. *Lines of Country: An Atlas of Railway and Waterway History in Canada*. Erin, ON: Boston Mills Press, 1997.

Angus, F.F. "The Eightieth Anniversary of the Short Line." *Canadian Rail*, No. 211 (June 1969).

Ballantyne, Bruce, ed. *Canadian Railway Station Guide*. Ottawa: Bytown Railway Society Inc, 1998.

Booth, J.D. *The Quebec Central Railway: From the St. Francis to the Chaudiere*. Toronto: Railfare Books, 2006.

———. *The Railways of Southern Quebec: Volume II*. Toronto: Railfare Enterprises, 1982, 1985.

Bush, E.F. *Engine Houses and Turntables in Canada, 1850–1950*. Erin, ON: Boston Mills Press, 1999.

Cooper, Bruce Clement. *The Golden Age of Canadian Railways*. Stroud, Glouchestershire, UK: Boolcraft Ltd., 2010.

Middleton, William D. *The Bridge at Quebec*. Bloomington, IN: Indiana University Press, 2001.

Mika, Nick, Helma Mika, with Donald M. Wilson. *Illustrated History of Canadian Railways*. Belleville, ON: Mika Publishing Co., 1986.

Murray, Tom. *Rails Across Canada: History of the Canadian Pacific and Canadian National Railways*. UK: Voyageur Press, 2011.

Pieroway, Kenneth G. *Rails Across the Rock: A Then and Now Celebration of the Newfoundland Railway*. St. John's, NL: Creative Publishing, 2013.

Pratte, France Gagnon, and Eric Etter. *The Fairmont Chateau Frontenac*. Quebec: Editions Continuite Inc., 2012.

Roberts, Erle W., and David P. Stremes, eds. *Canadian Trackside Guide 2013*. Ottawa, ON: Bytown Railway Society, 2013.

Solomon, Briand. *North American Railroad Bridges*. St. Paul, MN: MBI Publishing Company and Voyageur Press, 2007.

"The Quebec Central Railway Sights and Scenes for the Tourist." Sherbrooke, QC: Pamphlet issued by the Passenger Department, 1889.

Wilkins, Robert N. "Dalhousie Square Rises From the Ashes." *Montreal Gazette*, October 12, 1913.

WEBSITES

"40th Anniversary of the Demolition of the Van Horne Mansion." www.heritagemontreal.org/en/40e-anniversaire-de-la-demolition-de-la-maison-van-horne.

"All Aboard, Exploring the Newfoundland Railway/ Coastal History." www.virtualmuseum.ca.

Ballentyne, Bruce. "Stations of the Gatineau Valley Railway." *Outaouais Heritage WebMagazine*. www.outaouais.quebec-heritageweb.com.

Boyko, Steve. "An Afternoon on the Napadogan." Confessions of a Train Geek. August 3, 2007. blog.traingeek.ca.

Ibid. "Napadogan Memories."

"The Branch Lines." www.heritage.nf.ca/society/Robertcuff.

"Canada Atlantic Railway." www.canada-rail.com/ontario/railways/CAR.html.

"Canadian Pacific's Tunnel at Wolfe's Cove, Quebec City." pages.globetrotter.net/burridge/WC_Tunnel.html.

"Canadian National Stations in Quebec." www.barraclou.com/stations/quebec.

"The Canadian Pacific Railway's Legendary Angus Shops." www.members.kos.net/sdgagnon/ang.html.

www.canadianrailwayobservations.com.

"A Canadian Regional Railroad, 1930s–1940s, Quebec Central Railway."www.r2parks.net/QC.html.

Churcher, Colin and Raymond Farand. "The Bridge Over the Ottawa River at Fitzroy." www.railways.incanada.net/articles/article2008_03.html.

"CN Shops in Point Saint Charles." www.heritagemontreal.org/en/cn-shops-in-point-st-charles.

Colin Churcher's Railway Pages. "The Union Forwarding Company Railway-the First Railway in the Ottawa Valley, The Horse Railway That Ran a Royal Train." www.railways.incanada.net/Articles/Articles2006_10.html.

"Cornwallis River Greenway." www.cornwallisgreenway.ca.

"Cycling the Estriade in Quebec's Eastern Townships." www.gobiking.ca.

www.cycloparcppj.org.

"Estriade Piste Cylclable du Quebec." www.estriade.net.

"Extant Railway Structures of New Brunswick." www.rshs.org.

Ibid. "Extant Railway Structures of Newfoundland."

Ibid. "Extant Railway Structures of Nova Scotia."

Ibid. "Extant Railway Structures of Prince Edward Island."

Ibid. "Extant Railway Structures of Quebec."

"Fairmont le Chateau Montebello, Hotel History." www.fairmont.com/montebello/hotel-history.

Farfan, Matthew. "Railway Stations of the Eastern Townships." *Townships Heritage WebMagazine*. www.townships-heritage.com/attraction/railway-stations-easterntownships.

"The First Railway to Aylmer." *Colin Churcher's Railway Pages*. www.railways.incanada.net/Articles/Articles_2004.4html.

"Gare de Cabano." www.historicplaces.ca/eng.

"Gare de Charny." www.patrimoineduquebec.com/gares/Charny.html.

"Une Gare Patrimoniale." www.garederivierebleue.com.

"Gibson, Alexander." *Dictionary of Canadian Biography*. www.biographi.ca/en/bio/Gibson_alexander_14E.html.

"Grand Trunk Bridge." www.memorablemontreal.com.

Ibid. "Victoria Bridge."

"Great Northern Railway of Canada." www.canada-rail.com/quebec/railways/GNR.html.

"The Great Saint John Steel Cantilever Bridge." www.johnwood1946.wordpress.com.

"Halifax and Southwestern Railway Museum, Lunenburg Nova Scotia." www.yourpictures.com/HSWRRailway.

"A Heritage Station." www.garederivierebleu.com/en/heritage-station.

"Historic Chignecto Ship Railway Lands Purchased." February 2012. www.novascotia.ca/natr/land/chignecto2012.

"L'Historique Gare de L'Epiphanie abandonee puis oubliee." www.hebdorivenord.com/economie/2010-01-19.

"History of Victoria Bridge, 1860." www.canadianrailwaytimes.com.

"Joffre Roundhouse." National Historic Site of Canada. www.historicplaces.ca/en.

Kennedy, R.L. "National Transcontinental Railway; Canada's Third Transcontinental Railway." www.trainweb.org/oldtimetrains.

"Kensington PEI, Railways." www.kennet.pe.ca/chip/english/railway.html.

"Key Railway Heritage Sites in Nova Scotia." www.novascotiarailwayheritage.com.

"Legrand Hotel Port Daniel." *Gaspesian Heritage WebMagazine*. www.gaspesie.quebecheritageweb.com/article/legrand-hotel.

"Le Massif de Charlevoix Train." www.lemassif.com.

Lemon, Wendell. "The Temiscouata Railway Company 1889-1948." www.trainweb.org/oldtimetrains.

"Ministers Island, National Historic Site of Canada." Parks Canada. www.pc.gc.ca.

"Nashwaak Trail." www.frederictontrailscoalition.com.

New Brunswick Railway Heritage Association. "Railway Sites."; "Other Sites of Interest." www.nbrailways.ca/html.

"New Brunswick Railway History." www.traingeek.ca.

"The Newfoundland Railway, 1882–1988." www.yourpictures.com/newfoundlandrailway.

"Newfoundland T'Railway Provincial Park." www.trailway.ca.

"Orangedale Station Architecture." www.novascotiarailwayheritage.com/Orangedale.

"Les Origines de la Cycloroute de Bellechasse." www.cycloroutebellechasse.com.

"Park Pays Tribute to Years of Marine and Rail Service." PEI News Release. September 4, 2000. www.gov.pe.ca/Newsroom

"Eastern Quebec Railways." *Patrick Sirois's Railway Website*. www.trainweb.org/trainmaster.

"Le Petit Guide du Triton." www.lapresse.ca/voyage/destinations/quebec/mauricie.

"Pier 21, National Historic Site of Canada." Parks Canada, www.pc.gc.ca.

"Pontiac Pacific Junction Railway, Shawville Station and the Pontiac Museum." *Outaouais Heritage WebMagazine*, www.outaouais.quebecheritageweb.com.

"Prince Edward Island Railway." www.canada-rail.com/maritimes/railways/PEIR.html.

"Quebec Bike Paths." www.out-there.com.

"Quebec City Rail Tours." www.viator.com/quebec-city-tours/rail-tours.

"Railway Heritage Sites Along the Lighthouse Route." www.novascotiarailwayheritage.com

"Railway Heritage Sites Along the Evangeline Trail." www.clarenville.newfoundland.ws/Clarenville-Railway-History.asp. Ibid. "The Railway in Clarenville 1891-1988."

"Two Railway Stations in the Historic City Centre." "The Railway Station District." www.vieux.montreal.qc.ca.

"Redevelopment of the Angus Site-Montreal Quebec." Canadian Mortgage and Housing Corporation. www.cmhc-schl.gc.ca/en/inpr/afhoc/afhoc/afhostcast.

www.reseaucharlevoix.com.

"Roads for Rails, the Closure of the Newfoundland Railway." www.heritage.nf.ca/society.

www.roddvacations.com/rodd-charlottetown.

"Roundhouse Action Group, the Kentville Roundhouse Was Demolished by the Town of Kentville on 9 July 2007." www.novascotiarailwayheritage.com/roundhouse_action_group.html.

"Sackville to Cape Tormentine, Trans Canada Trail." www.sentiernb.com.

"Saving the Ste Agathe Railway Station — Again." *Laurentian Heritage WebMagazine*. www.laurentian.quebecheritageweb.com/news/saving-ste-agathe-railway-station-again.

"La Seigneurie du Triton." www.seigneuriedutriton.com.

"Significant Dates in Nova Scotia Railway History." www.ns1978.ca/rail/sigdates-rail04.html.

St. John's Newfoundland. www.railwaycoastalmuseum.ca.

"Tidnish Bridge." www.historicplaces.ca/en.

"Train du Haut St Francois." www.grandquebec.com/cantons-est/train-touristique-st-francois.

Bibliography

"The Train Station Inn History." www.trainstation.ca/tatamagouche_railway_history.html.

"The Trinity Train Loop." www.historicplaces.ca/en.

"Van Horne/Shaugnessy House National historic Site of Canada." Parks Canada, www.pc.gc.ca.

"Velopiste Jacques Cartier-Portneuf." www.velocpistejcp.com.

INDEX

ALSO AVAILABLE FROM DUNDURN

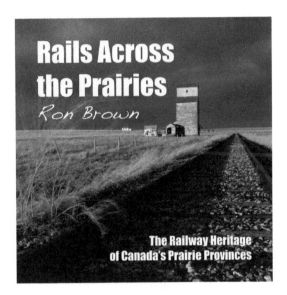

Rails Across the Prairies

Follow the evolution of the rail legacy of the Canadian Prairies from the arrival of the first engine on a barge to today's realities.

Rails Across the Prairies traces the evolution of Canada's rail network, including the appearance of the first steam engine on the back of a barge. The book looks at the arrival of European settlers before the railway and examines how they coped by using ferry services on the Assiniboine and North Saskatchewan Rivers. The work then follows the building of the railways, the rivalries of their owners, and the unusual irrigation works of Canadian Pacific Railway. The towns were nearly all the creation of the railways from their layout to their often unusual names.

Eventually, the rail lines declined, though many are experiencing a limited revival. Learn what the heritage lover can still see of the Prairies' railway legacy, including existing rail operations and the stories the railways brought with them. Many landmarks lie vacant, including ghost towns and elevators, while many others survive as museums or interpretive sites.

Georgina Public Libraries
90 Wexford Dr
Keswick, ON L4P 3P7

Available at your favourite bookseller

VISIT US AT

Dundurn.com
@dundurnpress
Facebook.com/dundurnpress
Pinterest.com/dundurnpress